Study Abroad

The Book of Jobe

Copyright © Jobe Leonard 2013

This book is sold subject to the condition that it shall not, by way of trade or otherwise, be lent, resold, hired out, or otherwise circulated without the publisher's prior consent in any form of binding or cover other than that in which it is published and without a similar condition, being imposed on the subsequent publisher.

For information about special discounts, bulk purchases, or autographed editions please contact Jobe Leonard at JobeLeonard@gmail.com

Write to:

Jobe Leonard Books
1511 Mayflower Lane
Dandridge, TN 37725

Or visit:

www.Jobe.ws

Or

www.Facebook.com/StudyAbroadBook

Or

@JobeLeonard on Twitter

Jobe Leonard
ISBN-13: 978-0615664088
ISBN-10: 0615664083

Introduction

This journal is a very different kind of literature. It is an intimate portrait of my daily experiences not filtered through any kind of editorial process. The intention is not to tell all of my life experiences, just those surrounding the time of each particular entry. All the same, autobiography, travel journal, and diary could be worthy descriptions of this piece.

This work is a true story in its entirety. Each event, hardship, and comical moment was experienced and recorded at the time indicated. My purpose in publishing this writing is to locate the acquaintances from my travels and share this piece of literature with them. I am in constant search of all the characters in this book. If you recognize any of the people in the book as yourself or someone you may know I would love to hear from you.

Study Abroad

30th August, 2004
11:30 p.m.

    I do not know quite what to expect, but I am ready to go. I will wake up at 8:00 a.m. tomorrow. I am going to the Nashville airport for a flight to Minneapolis. Then I am off to the Netherlands.

31st August, 2004
11:45 a.m.

    After months of preparation, I was finally about to board the plane. I kissed Mom and gave Dad a hug. Travel was nothing new after a senior trip, a few spring breaks, and many random breakneck road trips to beaches around the southeastern United States. I was certain I was an expert at the American auto-driven road trip. However, a foreign country presented a slight escalation of the word travel. No longer would a day, weekend, or even a week seem endless after a stay of this length.

31st August, 2004
5:17 p.m.

    I am in Minneapolis now. I had chips, salsa, and a Budweiser at Chili's. Ben and I are waiting for our flight to Amsterdam that leaves at 7:00 p.m. My spirits are high. I am ready to arrive in the Netherlands. I will then begin my study abroad.

31st August, 2004
11:45 p.m.

    I am flying over the Atlantic Ocean now. My friend Ben, with whom I will be studying abroad, is on the same flight. His seat is far away, but he is close enough where I can see him. The lady beside him has a very small baby but no daddy on the flight with her. Ben is currently holding the baby, feeding it, and possibly changing it. Airplane seating, like life, is such luck of the draw. Just when one thinks they have done all their research and chosen the best option, something like this happens.

1st September, 2004
8:10 a.m.

My plane is hovering over Amsterdam's Schipol airport and waiting to land. The flight was great, except I could not sleep. Coach is OK for a short flight, but I yearn to stretch my legs after being cramped in this uncomfortable seat for nine hours. Maybe I can catch up on my sleep one of these days in the Netherlands. I am filling out an immigration card to give to the customs agent, in Amsterdam. I have all my required documents, insurance, and bank statements ready just in case I am questioned.

1st September, 2004
1:30 p.m.

I walked through customs without a word from the agent. I received my European Union rubberstamp on a crisp new passport. My next plane ride from Amsterdam to Maastricht was exhilarating. The mini-airport we arrived at was the perfect size for the twin-prop plane that so graciously guided us on the last connection of our first journey of this study abroad.

Steven, a student from the university we will be attending, greeted us at the Maastricht airport. He drove us to our student housing. Once there, we unloaded our gear, finalized our lease, and received our keys. Not wanting to get jet lag, I was smart enough to know that staying awake and finding a decent bedtime later in the evening would be beneficial.

2nd September, 2004
3:22 a.m.

    Waking up at 2:30 a.m. in a foreign country is unnerving. I accidentally fell asleep at 2:00 in the afternoon. Here I sit, fully rested. I do not know a single fact about what is in the darkness outside of my apartment's glass sliding door, or what is to come in the approaching months. I am about to write letters to home, and I am eating a banana that strangely found its way to my desk.

    I have a nifty sink and shower room conveniently placed inside my apartment. One item is missing that needs to be addressed. My apartment is lacking a toilet. I entered a hallway outside my door. The hall has the slight odor of a closet, undisturbed. Four doors down was a commode. It had no water in the bowl. Like a curious 3 year-old I decided to do a test flush. The toilet's tank was not positioned as usual on top of the bowl. It was hanging on the wall behind the toilet at least seven feet in the air. I pulled a string that was connected to the tank, and a mighty waterfall of gravity-powered water flowed, swirled, and then disappeared.

    I left the bathroom and took a right through glass doors into my floor's dining area. This was also the kitchen that I imagined I would be sharing with the other nine apartments located in my hallway. The room contained a stove, two mini dorm fridges, a table with eight chairs, and nine wooden closet boxes that were under the security of lock and key. This would hold my non-refrigerated food. The size of my personal box suggested that it could hold what I estimated would be a week's worth of food if fully stocked.

    The only problem I had now was that I had no clue where a grocery store might be. Also, I could not read or speak a single word of the Dutch language. As I stare into my security box, I begin to wonder about who else is on my floor. Ben's apartment is right next door to mine, but both mini fridges are packed to the brim with food. I begin to investigate everyone else's refrigerated items so that I will know what items look like once I find a place to buy my own. After eating a pilfered piece of bread, drinking someone's orange juice, and nibbling on stolen cheese, I wanted to see my apartment room once again. Opening the door this time, I noticed my bed looking inquisitively at me. I decided to rest a bit more.

2nd September, 2004
8:34 a.m.

    With one eye open and rays of sunshine infiltrating my room, I noticed another item that would surely be a close companion over the coming months. The clouds outside of my apartment window were fluffy white and suspended in a big blue sky in a painted pattern. If I had a paintbrush and Van Gogh's skill, I could surely sketch the skies of Holland in an instant. I brushed my teeth and took a shower without soap. I am about to walk over to my neighbor's apartment.

    Ben and I are both 21-year-old seniors from Tennessee Technological University. In the university cafeteria during March of last year, he told me about a study abroad program he was applying for at an international business school in the Netherlands. I pressed him for additional details about the program. That night I called home I asked my mother her thoughts on studying abroad. She told me I was going to do it, and she mailed me the application fee. This effectively placed me on the same path as Ben. It seems surreal that I just spent my first night here.

2nd September, 2004
2:07 p.m.

After speaking with Ben this morning, we were both certain we had gone to bed too early. We also needed to find food, soap, and toothpaste. A five-mile walk put us in the city center of Sittard. We ate at a quaint restaurant with a floor of multi-century-old cobblestones. The sandwich I ordered at the restaurant contained an item that I detested, tomato. This Dutch tomato slice and I exchanged glances and called a permanent truce. I must say it was quite delicious, and I was starving.

Lunch was over, and it was now time for the grocery store. It was an Aldi, which I had never heard of before. This would truly be my first class of my study abroad, Grocery 101. The first lesson I learned was that beers are inexpensive and they are purchased individually. If I wanted three beers I could buy three beers. Then I noticed milk was not refrigerated. This turned my stomach a bit.

Finally apples, oranges, and bananas were identical to what I was used to. I decided that fruits were the safest shopping option for now.

    I gathered my beer, bread, cheese, and fruits. I placed them on the black rolling conveyor. They made their final descent to a cashier dressed like a pharmacist surrounded by a steel cage full of tobacco. She scanned my purchases and said something to me in Dutch. I did not comprehend. I just smiled, and I paid her according to the cash register's digital readout. Then I stuffed my purchases in my backpack while Ben checked out behind me.

    The true lesson of this first class came in transporting the groceries home. During the four-mile walk, I realized that anything I was going eat on a daily basis would have to be loaded in my backpack and carried back to my apartment. The days of getting into my automobile and driving wherever I pleased were officially over.

    On the way back to our apartment complex, we stopped in a liquor store. Our town, Sittard, is very near the borders of both Germany and Belgium. I was surprised to see how low the prices were. Jagermeister was less than half of what it would cost for the same bottle in Tennessee. More amazing to me was that Jack Daniel's also costs less here in Holland than it does in Tennessee. How could it be possible that a company could ship a bottle of liquid thousands of miles and still sell it for less than what it costs 100 miles away from its manufacturing facility? Cheers to taxes. Cheers to classes. I have my orientation at the university tomorrow at 1:30 p.m.

3rd September, 2004
8:30 p.m.

I have slept very well since I have been here, and I hope it continues. I woke up and wrote postcards to my parents and my friends back at Tennessee Tech. Today was my first day of class and orientation. There are 20 other exchange students from a variety of countries.

For my curriculum I signed up for 18 hours of classes instead of my required 12. This way I will have a buffer if one of the classes does not go as planned. I am graduating in May, and I do not want this semester abroad to force me to stay in school any longer. I also will go to the university often so I can socialize and use the Internet. Why not take a few extra classes and learn while I am on campus?

6th September, 2004
2:45 p.m.

After three days of grocery shopping, meeting my classmates, and exploring the town I was back at the university today. The meetings of each class could be few and far between. A three-hour course that would have met three times a week at Tennessee Tech will meet once a week here. Each class is also subject to cancellation without a makeup date. I imagined that this is because the teachers here are professionals in their respective fields.

    In accounting class, an accountant from a local firm will teach us. For marketing, the president of an advertising agency will direct our class. The school uses these teachers to give us real-life perspectives. Each school should use someone who has actually practiced the profession. Some professors in the United States seemed like they were overpaid and over-educated. The only thing they brought to class was a curriculum that had remained unchanged for the past 20 years. One negative side of the proposition was that the Dutch teachers did have professional commitments. These priorities might take precedence over our instructional sessions. I should be able to forgive them for this.

6th September, 2004
10:48 p.m.

    I went to the town square tonight with a group of students from my class that consisted of three French, three Hungarians, four Americans, two Dutch, one German, six Chinese, two Finnish, and one Polish student. Ben and I went grocery shopping on the way there. The initial beers we ordered were lukewarm like the service. We began reaching into our backpacks and using our supplies to refill our glasses.

    I also spoke to the other American students - Bryan, Brett, and Mallory - about the student visas we needed to live in the Netherlands. Today was our last day to register with the local authorities. The cost of a visa was around 500 Euros. After a brief discussion with my American classmates, I decided I was going to risk it. This meant if the police stopped me for any reason, I would be deported. It should be a very interesting semester living as an illegal alien in the Netherlands.

6th September, 2004
1:07 p.m.

Right now I am sitting in Business Enterprises class. I have met a few more new companions. To ease the retention of the names I will most likely refer to each of them by their nationalities. I will only speak singularly about them when absolutely necessary. With this many counterparts my semester should play out like an international version of MTV's "Real World."

In Sittard a large majority of my group, including me, lives in a most special and unique place. My apartment complex's official name is Watersley. It was one of those places that no matter how it was pronounced, it needed correction from a local. Try each of these acceptable pronunciations: Watersley, Water-Sleigh, Waters-Lee, Vaterslay, Voaterslee, etc. None would be deemed correct if I said it. However, it would be replaced with one from the list when I was corrected. I am sure this correction was because we were immigrants. Also, the locals were dumbfounded that we lived at Watersley.

After the first few days here, asking questions and observing my surroundings I have come to the conclusion that Watersley was not actually student housing. Its primary purpose is a compound for the mentally handicapped. They had opened a few vacant floors for student housing several years ago. The individuals who resided on the property ranged from mildly mentally handicapped to extremely impaired persons in straightjackets. The further I went into the woods of the compound is where the howls and screams could sometimes be heard. After a few days living here I am coming to the realization that I could live in any place, anywhere, around the globe.

**7th September, 2004
3:00 p.m.**

Today is laundry day. It is time for laundry because all the walking and sweating I have done over the past week have left me with a large pile of dirty clothes. The cost of the machines in our building is three euros for a load that must be about a quarter of what a good American Maytag washing machine can hold. I hand washed clothes in my apartment's sink, and then I hung them on my porch and in my room on clotheslines I made from a spool of rope.

I simply cannot wait until I can get a bicycle. My feet hurt so much from the 10-mile roundtrip to the grocery store, and an 18-mile round-trip to class. Hopefully tomorrow a new bike will finally happen.

**8th September, 2004
8:23 p.m.**

    Oh, another day, and this is my first chance to sit down after quite a long day. Ben and I started our walk to class at 8:30 a.m. in the pouring rain. We wanted to get to campus early. We could use the Internet to send e-mails to America, before class. After our two classes, which went great, we went to finally purchase a bike.

    First, I called a Dutch gentleman whose name and number we had been given. He was a local bike dealer. He was supposed to sell Ben and me a bike a week ago.

    "I only have two or three bikes ready. Can you come by tomorrow?" The bike dealer said.

    "I only want one bike," I informed him. "I am sure I can make do with what you have. The arches on my feet have flattened out. My calves cramp when I sleep from walking so damn much."

    He lectured me. "You must wait until tomorrow at 11:00 a.m."

    Forty-five minutes later, I am at a bike store underneath the train station with Ben. I have been to this bicycle shop before, but everything was overpriced. We tell the clerk we are from Great Britain, for some reason. Then we tell him we want a bike whose price is 50 euros or less. He leads us to a back room of the bike shop with six or seven bikes that have not had their repairs paid for, after they were dropped off.

    Ben had trouble finding one he liked. I rode three or four bikes around the shop and then I happened across a 1976, white, Raleigh classic road bike for 25 euros. Ben found a non-repair-room special and paid about 100 euros. We entered the bike store on tired, aching feet and left riding our steel horses with renewed vigor and freedom.

    The infrastructure in the Netherlands was developed with a cyclist in mind. Every building, bar, and store had bike racks out front for parking. The streets had an intricate system of bicycle highways, lanes, bike signs, and stoplights to make every journey easy. The Dutch landscape was completely flat except for the massive mountain that Watersley was located on. With our new mobility, we located a McDonald's and had a snack. Then we visited a movie theater and finished off the day at an Irish pub. None of these trips was possible on foot, but on a bike we could handle them all in an afternoon.

    After walking for days on end, one would not know how appreciated it was to finally have wheels. Not wheels like the American teen would find on a 16th birthday, but wheels like a 6 year-old might find on his birthday. A bike in the past had been a tool of my childhood that allowed me to terrorize the neighborhood and break several local land-speed records with a tin can wrapped around my back wheel to make it sound like a motorcycle. Now this bicycle was my legs. It would take me to class, to get groceries, and to the train station. It satisfied any and all of my needs.

    After the first day of riding, I could tell a difference in my legs' muscle tone. My calves were already becoming somewhat sculpted from walking 20-plus miles per day over the past week. I now have one day of cycling and traversing the bike roads under my belt.

Ben and I plan to take a trip to Maastricht tomorrow, in the morning. We want to give our bicycles a test run. It is about 27 miles each way, so it should be an interesting trip.

9th September, 2004
8:49 p.m.

The test ride to Maastricht was great. We began shortly after class at 10:30 a.m. We stopped at a sister university of the one we attend in Sittard. This is where Mr. Burt Kamphius worked. He was our contact in the Netherlands before we arrived, and he met us at Watersley on our first day to make sure everything with our check-in went smoothly.

Shock would be a mild word for how he we reacted when we told him we bicycled to his office. I guess even in a country where bicycling is common, a 27-mile one-way trip is a bit too far. If someone should doubt this, try it.

After exploring the Maastricht city center, and facing the daunting ride back and near dusk, we decided to take the train. We loaded our bikes onto the train car that allowed bikes. The three-hour journey by bike was shortened to 12 minutes on the train.

10th September, 2004
1:13 p.m.

    I am working on homework for my Logistics class. I am certain I need to buy another 100-euro textbook. I guess it is really not much different from an American university. I am feeling a monetary squeeze of having a limited budget. I have plenty of money, but once it is gone there is no way to get more. Even if I wanted to work somewhere, I could not. I do not have a student visa or a work visa.

11th September, 2004
11:32 a.m.

    I am done with my first week of class and homework. I am enjoying my weekend, in the community room at Watersley, watching European television. Last night we ate Mexican food for dinner and watched one of the Indiana Jones movies on the television. It was the first time I had viewed it, and probably the last, unless they rerun it. This movie on TV did not have a single commercial. They played the movie in English with Dutch subtitles. This also helps the Dutch population learn English, and they speak, write, and read it really well.
    We finished the movie last night. Maxime and I went down to the town center via our bikes. We went to a bar in the middle of the square and had a glass of Grolsh beer. Then we went next door and drank two more beers. One was paid for. The next was from the bartender for free.

Suddenly a blond, curly haired man with a brown mustache walks in. He strolled quickly to the back room of the bar. Moments later he walked back out. He was about to leave.

"Nightwatcher!" The bartender yelled, "An American and a Frenchman are beside you drinking."

The blond, curly haired man laughed. The United States had wars taking place in Iraq and Afghanistan. We were in an era of French and American animosity. Max and I were not supposed to agree on anything, or God forbid, enjoy a drink together at a bar. The leaving patron abruptly yelled to the bartender.

He said, "Get me and these gentleman something to drink. Make it something the French and Americans can agree on. Bring us three shots of German Jager and three Dutch Heineken beers."

We introduced ourselves. He told us his name was the Nightwatcher. He told us that anytime we met him in Sittard he would provide us with free drinks. It is now four beers later, and I believe him about the free-drink thing. With a good buzz going, the Nightwatcher pays his and our tabs. He walks out the door.

I start a light-hearted conversation with Max. We talked about the similarities and differences of our two countries. He then got extremely serious and asked me a question. Max asked if I knew a gentleman named Shuck Morise. The French accent made this man sound very intriguing as Max told me stories of him riding on horseback, taking criminals into custody, and saving women in distress. I was amazed and listened in awe. Max told me the story of this modern-day hero who freed the countryside of crime. Then Max asked me if I had heard of him, and I had not. He was amazed I knew nothing of him.

"Shuck Morise zey teckass rangair," Max said with a French accent.

"Chuck Norris!" I exclaimed. This one bar visit on a crisp fall evening had birthed a larger-than-life hero, and a friendship was no doubt cemented by Chuck Norris, the Nightwatcher, Jager, and a few gallons of Dutch beer.

**12th September, 2004
7:30 p.m.**

This weekend we went to the beach in Den Haag. My friends from Finland, Liisa and Eeva, had invited me on this trip. This was my first weekend trip. We went by train to Den Haag. It was Ben, Eeva, Liisa, Mallory, and I. We rented a hostel room close to the train station and proceeded to Schevinegen. This was where the beach was located.

The Netherlands held European Union presidency. All the representatives for each country in the European Union were in The Hague. We sat on the beach in front of a spaceship-looking pier. While we were lying there, TV crews covering the summit in the building behind us routinely swept by our towels. They were filming the building behind us that held all the diplomats and their flags, just hoping to catch a glimpse of the representatives. Ben and I had forgotten shorts and swimsuits. We hunkered down on the white sand with no shirts and blue jeans rolled up to our knees for relaxation with the Finnish girls.

A quick trip to the pier for a bottle of water revealed a casino tucked inside. We gave the cashier 10 euros a piece for chips and proceeded to play. I lost it quickly. I then walked over to Ben, who had one coin left. Ka-ching, the screen swirls, click, click, click, Jackpot! A screen popped up with instructions. The only issue was that the screen was in Dutch. Ben pressed the least offensive-looking Dutch word on the touch screen. He received a bonus play. Nothing lined up on this spin. Something was different. There was no more money in Ben's jackpot. He had just accidentally bet it all on his attempt to cash out.

How many times do we hit jackpots in life only to spin them away by not understanding the consequences of our next action and going double down in the wrong direction? My friend Ben, who is an accounting wizard, looked at me, disappointed. I told him the loss was all on paper, and we walked back to our beach towels.

After a long day at the beach, we accidentally found an Irish steakhouse, The Fiddler. I was quickly learning that during international travel the English speakers of the world congregate at Irish pubs. Even in the worst-case scenario there will be at least one English speaker, the bartender. We found this pub and eatery to be full of Australian, English, and American patrons. The menu was also in English. After weeks of not knowing what I was ordering, it was welcome.

I tried the shepard's pie, which was heavenly, and the Guinness was just thick enough to fill the remaining void. We paid our tabs and walked back to the hostel to call it a night.

  This morning we took a two-hour train ride back home. How could a place thousands of miles away feel like home after only two weeks? What was home now? Was it the place I knew I was supposed to spend a majority of my nights, or just the place where a majority of my possessions resided? After returning from a weekend trip to Den Haag, Watersley already felt like home. I was coming home, and even with the crazy people screaming bloody murder it was still the place I parked my bike, brushed my teeth, and kept my pillow.

13th September, 2004
10:50 p.m.

  All I have to say is that I love my bicycle. It has allowed me to begin visiting my classmates. Eszter, Gina, and Nora are Hungarian girls. Their French roommate, Max, and another American, Brett, all live together in a house on the other side of Sittard. All the Hungarian girls cook, clean, and treat me like a king. One of them plays the guitar while the others sing. They all like tea, cigarettes, and a yogurt candy called yogi-bon bons.

  Nora and I share the same birthday. We have blue eyes and brown hair. Our nickname is "twin brother and twin sister."

Brett is their American roommate, so he helped me early on with the translations while we were still learning the Hungarian and French-speaking intricacies.

14th September, 2004
11:29 p.m.

    I rode my bike to school this morning alongside Bryan. He lives two floors down from me. We had conversations about the day-to-day grind of living in a psych ward. We are not at Watersley because of our mental capacities but more for the need for affordable housing. With a price tag of just over 250 euros per month including utilities, we had it made.

    Bryan and I shared a zest for constant and vigorous travel. Bryan had backpacked Europe the entire summer before our semester began. He possessed a wealth of knowledge on train schedules and cheap plane tickets, and an ability to do anything without the slightest hint of embarrassment. All these are valuable skills for any rookie traveler on a journey as intense as this. I quickly found out that we both were in close sight of graduation.

    We met initially in the shared kitchen of Watersley a few weeks before. Our class schedule was similar. On our bike ride to school, we put together what would become the best bike route known to man. This could get us from Watersley to the university in record time with only one stop. Momentum is paramount in many of life's challenges, including riding a bicycle.

After our day at school, we rode back to Watersley. I have told stories before of the hill that Watersley sits upon. To explain it just once does it no justice. This hill is like a three-day workout in one hill. It is so steep Burt Kamphius warned us about a girl from three years ago who did not check her brakes before going down the hill. She was still in a coma, a condition we hoped to avoid although we already had excellent accommodations at Watersley.

15th September, 2004
10:37 p.m.

Today I did laundry in my room again. Then I went to find beer for a birthday party. Paul was from Poland, and we were having his birthday party at Watersley. We ended up in Germany to get the beer. We purchased it and came back and enjoyed the festivities. Now it is time to study. This is complicated by the fact that my books have not arrived yet. Oh well, no one else in my classes has received theirs either.

16th September, 2004
11:39 p.m.

I had three classes today. These included Logistics, Information Systems Four, Marketing, and my first class of Social Dutch. "Ik ben Jobe" is the Dutch equivalent of, "My name is Jobe." I could hope to write an entire journal entry in Dutch before I go back to the United States. After class, we made American food at the Hungarians house. Everyone enjoyed it, and we biked back home.

I just finished folding my laundry from yesterday. The scenery is different here, but the chores are the same. I need to write postcards and send a package. Tomorrow I have no class. Maybe I will stop by the post office then. This weekend looks like I might catch a soccer match in Rotterdam. Tomorrow we are going to play American football in the park with Max, Ben, Bryan, and Brett.

17th September, 2004
9:30 p.m.

I am ready to go to class. This afternoon I worked on my Risk Management paper about McDonald's for class. I also had soup for lunch. Class was good, but it is starting to get cold outside, and it is raining now. The 20-mile bike rides are horrible in this kind of weather.

My marketing teacher, Mr. Spaubeck, is a bit crazy. I am sure he thinks the same of me. I think he should use our marketing class as a target group. He can then take our ideas and use them in his marketing firm. Where else could he find a multinational panel of 18-to 22-year olds to survey?

18th September, 2004
10:39 p.m.

I traveled to Rotterdam with Brett and Ben today, which should make for an exciting weekend. My second week of class is now over. I am fully adjusted to the university's class style. Now I am just relaxing at a hostel in Rotterdam.

We met up with Bryan's friend Caroline in Rotterdam. Bryan had befriended her earlier this summer and gave us her phone number for our trip to Rotterdam. She grew up here and works as a dance instructor. She invited us into her home, and we had meatloaf, salad, and Heineken. I have no clue what we will get into tomorrow, but I need to go to the ATM. Being on the road is expensive, not to mention tiring.

**19th September, 2004
4:30 p.m.**

Surprise! I am riding back to Sittard from Amsterdam. Yesterday, when I woke up Ben, Brett, and I decided that we would pack up and move our reservation to Amsterdam. We had seen all we needed to see of Rotterdam.

We arrived in Amsterdam at noon and checked into the hostel. We made our way to the Van Gogh museum. I hated it. I do not know how many more museums I will go to. I know one thing for sure; It will not be my idea. Museums are truly not my cup of tea.

We moved our expedition to the Heineken Experience for a tour of the brewery. We met a group of American girls there. They were in Amsterdam for the weekend, too. The tour was a great time. We sampled three free beers on the tour. We also received a free souvenir glass as a gift.

After the Heineken museum, we bought tickets to an improvisational comedy show, Boom Chicago. The American girls we met at Heineken went with us, and it was a funny show. Then we used the buddy system. All seven of us took a walk through the red-light district and several other locations. We made it back to the hostel around 3:00 a.m. Then we went to bed.

In the morning we had breakfast and proceeded to take a boat tour through the canals. It was splendid, and we met three Croatian girls who were there on a business trip for Proctor & Gamble. After the boat trip we hoofed it to the Anne Frank house. Then we got on the train, and I am heading back to Sittard.

20th September, 2004
12:30 p.m.

I got a haircut today at Frankie's. He was an interesting Dutch hairstylist. His shop was small. It was filled with cigarette smoke, and the waiting room had Penthouse magazines on the table. It was now my turn.

"Do you want your haircut the old-fashioned way, like you have it? Or more trendy, my friend?" Frankie asked me with a bingo ash cigarette bouncing on his lip.

I thought to myself, if trendy is the way Frankie does his hair, no thanks. I proceeded to get my old-fashioned style haircut. To make a long story short, it looked great. It turned out that Frankie had won a hair-design contest in Paris years ago and used the money to start this shop in Sittard.

I will forever wonder what exactly he would have done with my hair had I gone for the trendy Frankie special.

22nd September, 2004
1:30 p.m.

Today I went to school early because I had a huge assignment due. The task was a four-page essay on the risks of a company for my Risk Management class. I had worked on it before, but now it was crunch time. The paper was due today at 10:30 a.m. I needed to proofread my paper. I did that and created my work-cited page.

Everything was complete until I turned to the cover sheet. The paper was missing a title. What would I call this masterpiece? My Risk Management assignment was on McDonald's and the corporate risks they face. Of the million-plus risks they have, I chose to write about two; health and environmental risks.

I looked around the computer lab at 7:30 a.m. I pondered a name for my first written assignment at my Dutch university. Then it came to me; "McRisk", that was it. I keyed it into the keyboard and centered it on the page, "McRisk". Even if this paper were four pages of garbage, a clever name like this would surely wow my professor, or maybe qualify me for a Nobel Prize in literature.

23rd September, 2004
A letter from home:

"Nobody nose you like your Mom." (On a card with two seals rubbing noses.)

Miss you, Thinking of you every day with Love. Know you are enjoying life there. Have fun and do some studying. See letter.

Love, Mom.

(Letter)
Hi Jobe,

    Sorry I did not write sooner. I wanted to write you ever since we received your letter and postcard. Thanks for doing so good in keeping in touch. Phone calls, letters, postcards, and e-mails. I am buying an international phone card this weekend so I can call you. Everyone is fine here and I really do not have too much news.
    Homecoming at Jefferson County High School is tomorrow, and we play Cocke County. Students are a bit lacking in spirit this year. Only ten teachers even bothered to decorate a homecoming door. Of course we did and it maybe another first place effort. HOSA is trying for the Spirit Award again. This would make four years in a row. I will let you know how we do.
    How is your bike doing? I bet you are getting a lot of good exercise and fresh air. How do you like your classes and professors? Are you and Ben eating well? You have met interesting characters, I suppose. It looks

like a very pleasant and beautiful place to live.

It was a close game with the Florida Gators last week. The University of Tennessee Vols pulled it out. Wilhite, the kicker, went from goat to hero. I am happy for all of them, and it will be their homecoming this week too.

The weather here this past week has been perfectly beautiful, no clouds, blue sky, cool nights, and warm days. It was a real shame to have to work during the most wonderful weather days of the year.

Your sister Kim came home last weekend and babysat. She might come home this weekend too. Peggy has been suffering from a sore throat the past two weeks and got on an antibiotic but it did not help. So now she got tested for Mono. I will find out later today. Hope not. The animals are fine. Scratching a few fleas, but the entire zoo is doing well and getting along.

Just going to finish up so I can pop this in the mail. We won first place for the homecoming door decoration contest. We will know at the pep rally today if we won the Spirit Award again this year. I read your e-mail to Dad yesterday and it was good to hear from you. I will be calling you really soon, sweetie. Be good, or as good as you can be. I will try to behave too! Go Big Orange! Go Patriots! Go Jobe and Ben, up the road on those Bikes! Zoom-zoom-zoomero!

Love Always,

Your Mama

24th, September, 2004
11:21 a.m.

    I am off class for the weekend. I have been thinking of taking a break in Aachen, Germany. This will be my first trip by myself. It should be a good time. Earlier today I went to save my pictures from Rotterdam and Amsterdam on Ben's computer to free up memory on my camera for the trip. I accidentally deleted all 106 of them instead, a true tragedy.

    Last night I had Jager Bombs made of Red Bull & Jager. Well kind of, we actually invented a new drink. The Aldi here in town has a generic Red Bull called Golden Power. It tastes the exact same. I can buy four Golden Powers for one euro. Red Bull's price is around three euros each. We called the new Jager Bombs made with Golden Power a Golden Shower.

25th September, 2004
4:03 p.m.

    I just got back from Aachen, Germany, and it was a great time. It cost me seven euros for the train rides to get there and back. My room was 21 euros. I walked to the hostel from the train station. Once there, I met one of my roommates. He was in the room with me. His name was Henry, and he was from Argentina. I took off my backpack and headed to Aachen's city center for the afternoon. I stayed in town all afternoon and quickly began to feel like a German.

I had a typical German lunch at McDonald's then walked to the park. Sitting in the park, I have come to the conclusion that I still crave American-branded food chains. I am beginning to see it as my only source of high-protein, high-calorie, high-fat rations. This type of diet is just not available at a typical European restaurant or my kitchen at Watersley. Eating delicious cheeseburgers makes me feel like Mario from Mario Brothers, after he has just found a mushroom.

After the park I went back to the hostel. At the hostel I found a television, I watched "Who Wants To Be a Millionaire" and "The King of Queens," in German. The T.V. was at the bar, so I sampled a beer and a pizza. Halfway into my meal, people started trickling in. The people kept coming and coming until the bar area for 12-15 people was packed with over 50 people. I was not feeling very social so I went into chameleon mode. I do this by not speaking unless absolutely necessary, because my English would give me away.

I tolerated the crowd for another 15 minutes then paid my tab and went towards the stairs to my room. The hallway was even more packed than the bar. Everyone was in a wheelchair. Apparently, all the congestion at the bar and at the stairs was caused by the fact that someone had booked a handicap convention at an establishment that was not handicap accessible. The hotel had guestrooms on the second floor only, and no elevator. I excused my way through the wheelchairs and hover-rounds as they looked at the daunting stairs. Then I stepped my way up the two flights of stairs and over to my room.

In my room I met more of my roommates. All of them were German university students. There were six German girls and Henry and I. We decided to go into town once more. I led the way since I had walked there earlier in the day. There were bands in the town center and a Mexican cantina, strangely enough. We had drinks and danced to the live music. We made it back around 1:00 a.m. At our hostel we brushed our teeth and went to bed.

The next morning I awoke bright and early. I walked to the train station at 8:30 a.m. I picked up an apple and nuts at a gas station. While waiting on my train at the Aachen station, I met a Nicaraguan man who spoke amazingly good English. He was headed to Den Haag, which I had just visited a week or so before. I helped him with directions, tickets, and which stations to get off at.

26th September, 2004
10:38 p.m.

I met up today with the Hungarian girls and Max at their place. They are simply the nicest people on the planet. Their home has been a great place to socialize. They serve delicious Hungarian dishes and always greet me with a kiss on the cheek.

My southern Appalachian accent was obviously difficult to translate from the

Queen's English they had learned. This could lead to a multitude of miscommunications. I would have to remember to fully connect and listen whenever something was said, or risk misinterpretation.

28th September, 2004
6:47 p.m.

Being in Holland makes it hard to avoid random Dutch people. The Dutch students I have befriended are named Christian and Steven. There is also a nurse who works at Watersley, and her name is Kim.

A typical Dutch student in their twenties has probably rarely or never driven a car. They may not even know how to back out of a driveway in one. We helped a Dutch student's family move today. His father had to back the family car out of the driveway so that we could get a couch outside. At 21 years old the Dutch student did not possess the ability to do this. I am certain he could have ridden a 15-mile wheelie to town on his bicycle, blindfolded, and standing on his handlebars if he needed to.

The Dutch students' knack for asking me to speak English is amazingly similar to an American's desire to hear Mexicans speak English in the United States. The only difference is their inability to notice that I was the illegal immigrant, and I should be the one speaking Dutch.

Due to recent heightened security and the increased cost of background checks, the cost of a visa for a student to study in the Netherlands is now triple what it was the year before. All the American students I studied with chose to skip out on the visa and beg for forgiveness if we were ever caught on the wrong side of the law. A simple traffic stop on my bicycle could have resulted in deportation. I now had an idea of what an illegal immigrant felt like in the United States, knowing they could be deported at any time for not having a proper visa.

**29th September, 2004
1:30 p.m.**

Lunch at school is my favorite. For two euros a day I can get a drink, soup, and fresh-made roll. Sometimes I find myself riding to school just for the soup. This is probably one of the reasons I can now see my hipbones and none of my pants fit anymore. A 20-mile bike ride for a cup of soup is not exactly an even calorie trade. Special soups like neon-green split pea, chicken noodle, and mystery stew made the trip worth it even if it was just to socialize, use the Internet, or meet with one of my class groups.

**30th, September, 2004
10:30 p.m.**

I have a big trip for this weekend that I have not mentioned yet. Dublin, Ireland. I am going with Ben and Mallory, then we will meet Brett there as well. We do not have much planned for when we get there, as of yet.

1st, October, 2004
7:30 a.m.

Hello, October I am sitting in the Brussels South Charleroi airport. We are about to depart for Dublin. We stayed in Leige' last night. It was nice, but we had to wake up at 4:00 a.m. to take the taxi to the train to the bus to the plane. Dublin should be fun.

Mallory is having a hard time with communication here in Belgium. She tried to pay a 1.50-euro bus fare with a 50-euro note and the bus driver could not make change.

"I cannot understand him, he speaks French." Mallory yelled across the bus.

I was thinking, "come on, Mallory, we are in Belgium." Oh well, I am sure she is out of her comfort zone just as much as I am.

2nd October, 2004
8:32 a.m.

Just waking up and slowly recalling what went on yesterday, so bear with me. We started off at the airport and checked into our hostel here in Dublin. We saved money and stayed in a room with 56 bunkbeds. We reasoned we would not be in the room much anyway. We checked in and claimed our beds.

First, we went to Trinity College, which is supposed to be one of the world's oldest. Then we went to the Guinness brewery. Along the way we picked up Brett, who had spent the previous week touring Northern Ireland. We toured the Guinness brewery. After the tour we received seven free Guinness beers at the brewery's sky bar, which overlooks the city.

On our way back to the hostel we signed up for a pub-crawl that started at 8:00 p.m. We had a bite to eat for dinner and then we made our way to the meeting place for the Dublin pub-crawl. We arrived at the meeting place at 7:45 p.m. We had our ten euros ready to cover the cost of the crawl. Other people who had signed up began to appear, and before long there were twenty-five people there. Only one problem: It was now 8:15 p.m. The pub-crawl group leader never showed up.

We considered heading back to the hostel, and then I had an idea. I yelled out to the group. What I told them was that even though the leader had not showed up, we could do our own pub-crawl and save our 10 euros. This group of 25 strangers, bound only by a common pub-crawl flyer and a desire to see Dublin's bars, set off on a monumental journey. We visited many bars and had laughs, beers, and good times.

The one thing I noticed about Dublin's bars is that they stink. It seems that they had recently banned smoking in the pubs. My theory is that over the last two hundred years the actual smell of Dublin's bars had been masked by cigarette smoke. The patrons drink their Guinness and Murphy's, and the thick beer gives them the worst rotten-egg sulfur farts.

I suspect that after so many years of being able to rip one inside the bar everyone got used to just lighting a cigarette. Then they would be able to hide the gas under the thick cloud of smoke. Today, with no smoking in the bars it can get downright atrocious. With seventy-five people in a bar all passing gas there were times when I just gagged a bit and threw up inside my mouth. My bar-fart theory might be the only downside to the new legislation on banning smoking in bars, especially in Dublin.

3rd October, 2004
2:34 p.m.

    This weekend was awesome. Now I am riding back from Maastricht on the train. Yesterday, we were so hungover from our pub-crawl that we took a senior citizen bus tour of the Irish countryside. We went to a town called Wicklow. On the way we visited the field that "Braveheart" was filmed on. Most of the day we rode on a nice air-conditioned bus in comfy seats. It was all we could muster.
    After a day of recuperation, we went for dinner and drinks. It turned out that the place we picked had American football on television. It was the 2nd of October and this was the first time I had been able to watch football all season. Amazing. The game at this bar was not the Vols, but it was an SEC match-up of LSU versus Georgia.
    We were watching the game and these cute girls kept walking by our table to go outside and smoke, or maybe they were just crop dusting. The third time they passed by I engaged them in conversation. They spoke English very well, and they were attending a private bachelorette party. They had rented the entire upstairs. This explained the cat

ears and pink ballerina tutus they were wearing.

After a few minutes of light chitchat they invited us upstairs to join their party. We crested the last stairs of the lofted bar and quickly realized we were right in the middle of wild Irish hen party. The maid of honor was shooting whiskey in the center of the party from the middle of her friend's tits. In addition, she was holding up a blow-up doll and dancing like an Irish wild woman.

Ben and I exchanged a glance. We looked at each other and listened. There was tons of noise going on from the group, but no one was talking. Everyone was using their hands. We both realized in the same instant that this group of thirty girls was deaf. Without hesitation I ordered a round of Jack and Cokes for everyone in the group and personally delivered the bride a glass of special congratulations from Tennessee.

The girls that we had initially met were very good lip readers, so we continued talking to them. They told us that everyone in their group went to a school for deaf girls in Dublin. Then they invited us to come to the after-party with them. Now the night was drawing to an end at this location, but even deaf girls like to dance.

We walked down the street as the only two guys in a group of over two dozen girls in typical bachelorette gear with dildos and blow-up dolls, screaming and raising hell. We finally made it to a club, and the first of the girls got in line. I watched.

"It's ten euros for the cover." The bouncer said to the deaf girls repeatedly.

With the entire group being deaf, they never picked up on it. Finally, after five minutes the line was amazingly long. The bouncer was frustrated. He let the entire group in. It was my turn in line. I faced the bouncer, and I looked him square in the eye. I did my best grunt, slapped my hands together, and walked in free of charge, too.

4th October, 2004
10:27 p.m.

I am back in Sittard and getting settled into class. All my grades are superb so far. This weekend Ben and I are going to visit Pisa, and Cinque Terre in Italy. We fly out on Thursday.

6th October, 2004
6:30 p.m.

Right now I am getting packed for a trip. I am pumped about my Italy trip. It should be good traveling with Ben in contrast to a larger group. We have a hotel the first night in Pisa and the location is right next to the leaning tower. Ben has a plan to get us to Cinque Terre, which is supposed to be a series of hill towns along the Mediteranean and connected by a trail. I am not sure what to expect. I am just lying low and saving money this week. This way I can have a good trip to Italy.

7th October, 2004
11:00 p.m.

    Here I am, on the road again. Ben and I took our flight from Brussels to Pisa and then a cab to right in front of the leaning tower. Our hotel is literally right next door. We checked into the hotel and grabbed a bit of pizza. Yes, I know, pizza in Pisa, but we had to.
    Our plan is to wake up at 6:30 tomorrow morning. This time is before all the tourists arrive on a cavalcade of tour buses. Then we can snap our pictures in front of the tower at sunrise with no one else in the background. Directly from the tower, we will go to the train station and ride to the Cinque Terre. We will spend a night in Cinque Terre, followed by a final night in Pisa. Then we will catch our flight back on Sunday.

8th October, 2004
8:30 p.m.

    We woke up and made our photographs in front of the tower just in time. I snapped my second picture when the first eighteen buses of tourists rolled up and started snapping pictures. We walked from there to the train station, where we caught a train. We made it to Cinque Terre around 11:30 a.m. today, and we quickly found a room in Rio Magiorre. It was 20 euros each. With this deal I inherited a comfy air mattress on the floor of an apartment.
    It should make for some good sleep tonight, as we are very worn out. We hiked

the entire Cinque Terre trail today, took a swim in the Mediterranean, and then caught the train back to the first town on the trail, where our apartment is. When we got back we had two new roommates, an Australian girl and her mom. They have already eaten, so Ben and I went to the local grocery store. We picked up a bottle of Cinque Terre wine, fresh pasta, homemade pesto, and a few Peroni beers. The apartment we rented beds in has a kitchenette. We boiled water for pasta and toasted with a glass of wine. We also offered wine to the Australian ladies who were boarding with us. They took us up on it.

    Dinner is over and we are finishing off the last of our wine and beers. The Australian lady told us that the shops close at 7:30 p.m. If we plan on buying more drinks we would need to leave now because it is 7:20 p.m. In a mad dash, Ben and I head down the stairs and to the same grocery we bought dinner from earlier. We purchased half a dozen more Peronis just as the shop was closing and headed back down the street. These beers were the last ones in town. I was certain since the grocery-store lady just turned the open sign to closed in the store behind us.

    Along the street at a small cafe there were two girls finishing up dinner and having a carafe of wine. I approach them and ask if they want to come help us finish these newly acquired beers. They exchange a glance with each other, and next thing we know we are walking up the stairs with them to our room.

    On the walk up we made them guess where we are from. They guessed Italy. I took it as a compliment. Tennessee boys who have only been in Europe for less than forty days are already being mistaken for Europeans. These girls were twins from California. The sisters had just finished graduate school and were taking a backpacking trip through Europe that just happened to cross my path.

We are gathered around the rented room's kitchen table with the Australians and our two new friends. We enjoyed the Peronis, and the Australians could not quit laughing. They were amused at the fact we were gone roughly three minutes. When we returned, we brought back two more visitors. We all enjoyed wine and beer. I suddenly remembered something. I had two emergency flasks full of Jager in my backpack for just such an occasion. I got them out and we pounded shots until both flasks were empty.

The California girls were staying in the town of Vernazza, which at this time of day was only accessible by train, although we had hiked through there earlier. They invited us out for a bit of nightlife with them, so off we went.

9th October, 2004
1:30 p.m.

Well, last night was fun. After we left the room, we went to an oceanside terrace and drank wine. One of the California girls dropped her glass and broke it. Our waiter made her buy the broken wine glass, so we left.

Next, we went to a bar in Vernazza that the two California girls had frequented during their stay there. At 10:00 p.m. we had a decision to make. We could ride back to Rio Maggiore or stay in Vernazza at the bars and clubs, which closed down at 5:00 a.m. Then we could catch the first train back in the morning. We decided to be responsible and go back.

Somewhere along the walk back to the train, Ben and I decided that we would intentionally act like we missed the train so we could hang out and have fun in Vernazza. It was just a good atmosphere, and it had a bit more nightlife than Rio Maggiore. We sat on the train station bench and watched as the last train of the evening rolled out of town.

We showed back up at the bar 35 minutes after leaving to a hero's welcome. A slow clap instantly started. All of a sudden, the bar cheered. We raised our hands in acceptance. We were immediately re-introduced into our game of beer pong we dominated an hour before. We played all night, and left the bar only to watch the sunrise over the Mediterranean.

It is now 7:00 a.m. and we are on the train platform waiting for a train back to Rio Maggiore, where we rented a room in vain. We caught the train back and arrived at our room. The Australian and her mom were finishing breakfast. They found it comical that we were getting into our beds at 7:30 a.m. for a little shuteye.

I must have had my eyes closed for every bit of three minutes when our door busts open and a cleaning lady comes in fussing loudly in Italian.

"English," I said as I sat straight up.

"You were supposed to check out thirty minutes ago. Get out now!" she demanded.

We hurriedly packed our backpacks and went out the door. From there we went straight to the beach. This is where we lay down once more. After a bit of a nap, and then a swim, we are on the train back to Pisa. Once there we will find a room near the airport so we can get up and catch our 7 a.m. flight without incident.

11th October, 2004
11:00 a.m.

It is now Monday, and I am sitting in class. School is not as fun as the weekend that I spent in Italy. We had a good time in Cinque Terra. It was good food, a lot of fun, and beautiful scenery. I have over eighty pictures of the weekend. I am staying home this weekend to hang out with Bryan, Ben, and Max in town.

12th October, 2004
1:30 p.m.

Our fall break is in two weeks, and here is what we are planning. We have a full week. We are going to go to London first, then to Paris. From Paris we are going to fly to Rome. When we leave Rome, we are going to visit Venice and Florence. I am working on booking my tickets right now. Tonight we are hanging out at Watersley and are going to play cards with our student group and maybe watch a movie.

15th October, 2004
6:30 p.m.

I am done with class for another week. Bryan and I took a ten-minute bike ride to Germany today to get Jagermeister. We also bought a chessboard. On the way home from Germany, we stopped and played the inaugural game in a cow field along a bike path. He beat me, but I am sure it will not be the last chess match. We have spent plenty of weeknights over the past month playing gin rummy until 2 a.m., and now we can add chess to our list of activities.

16th October, 2004
4:30 p.m.

Tonight we are going with a group of twenty-five students to De Buren. We have discovered that after dark De Buren changes from a restaurant into a discotheque. They hide all the tables somewhere, and a DJ plays music. It gets so crowded they also charge us to use the bathroom.

17th October, 2004
2:34 p.m.

De Buren was a blast last night. After the party, we camped out on the floor at the Hungarians'. It is a closer bike ride home from the bar. With everyone dancing at De Buren it was about one thousand degrees. While I was waiting for the bathroom, I looked for a seat to rest in for a minute. I found a heating register like the ones used to heat an old house. It was by the bathroom and I propped myself on it. This register had probably been broken off the wall multiple times by people doing the same thing. They had since electrified it like a cattle fence, as a deterrent. I sat down about to pass out from the heat while waiting on the bathroom. I got a shock so bad I went into survival mode. I felt like the bleeding soldier on a video game who has been shot so many times his vision becomes blurry and he can only walk in a stumble. With my fuzzy eyesight I moved through the bar crowd of Dutch students pulsing to techno. I tried to find my way to the door, all the time wondering what would happen to me if I were to pass out. After all, I was an illegal alien, and I had not seen a hospital my entire time in Europe.

    Would my study-abroad experience end here in the back of an ambulance as the paramedics and police tried to identify me using a strange Tennessee driver's license? I was on the verge of falling down in the middle of the dance floor. Then I felt the cool breeze from an open door. I followed the cold draft, and I finally found the door. I was able to catch a breath of fresh air that rejuvenated me. I decided to call it a night and went next door to Snack Point and got a Beck's beer and fresh-cut French fries to help me recover.

    Tonight we are headed to Maastricht. They have a bar there that plays NFL football on Sundays. It is an Irish pub called the Shamrock. If all goes well, I will get to watch my second football game of the fall tonight. We will not be able to watch the entire game because the last train from Maastricht to

Sittard leaves around 11:30 p.m., but it should satisfy my appetite for American football.

**18th October, 2004
8:39 p.m.**

    I booked the last of my tickets for our fall break. It will be a good one. London, Paris, Rome, Venice, and Florence all in one week. I am pumped about going back to Italy. Last night we had a great time watching football. Any Sunday I am in town I am going to do it again. There were plenty of American students from universities in Maastricht. Plus the bartender's name is Sue, and she speaks fluent English. Last night after the football match was over we went back to the train station.
    While we were waiting on the platform, I had to use the bathroom. Our train had not arrived yet, so I hopped on a train that was sitting there. I walked back to the bathroom and unzipped. In the middle of my relief, I realized that the train was starting to move. The empty train I was on was being moved for the night to the train yard. I ran to the door and jumped and rolled onto the platform just as the train left the station. We made it back to Sittard's station without further incident and rode our bikes back to Watersley around 12:30 a.m.

20th October, 2004
11:15 a.m.

It is only a few more days until we leave on our fall-break trip. I am pumped up. We are taking a train to Eindhoven and flying from there to London. Ben knows a girl with whom he worked on an accounting job. She is doing an audit in London. We are planning to stay with her. We will be heading out for this adventure on Thursday.

21st October, 2004
4:45 p.m.

I am boarding a train with Ben. We are going to Eindhoven to catch our flight to London's Stansted airport. We will stay two nights in London with Ben's friend and meet up with Ben's brother Jason and his aunt tomorrow. They are coming over from the United States to join us on our trip.

On the second day, Ben is taking the tunnel to Paris. I am going to fly. Bryan is going to be in London, too. He is meeting his mom, his sister, and his grandmother there. Bryan and his family are on the same flight as I am when we go to Paris. I plan on going to meet Bryan on Saturday in London. We will go to the airport together.

Once we arrive in Paris, we are meeting the Hungarian girls on Saturday night. We have a full day of sightseeing in Paris planned on Sunday before we fly to Rome on Monday morning. Then we will tour Rome for a day before catching a train to Florence and then on to Venice where we fly out on Sunday, October 31st. This should be a fun trip.

22nd October, 2004
11:00 a.m.

    We arrived in London without any issues. We made our way to the Hilton, where we met up with Ben's friend in the lobby. We had drinks in the lobby bar and then went out around town to several pubs. One thing about London is that the bars close down rather early. I am almost certain we made it home by midnight.
    Ben's friend had to work this morning, but we got a complimentary fresh-cooked room-service breakfast that was the closest thing to the Waffle House I have had since I have been in Europe. It was absolutely delicious. Now we are off to meet Ben's brother and aunt. Then we will see Westminster Abby, Big Ben, and all the sights of London.

23rd October, 2004
11:30 p.m.

    This is the last day in London. I am off to Paris this afternoon. I double-checked the name of the hotel that I am sharing with Ben in Paris. I told his friend how much I appreciate her letting us stay in her swank room for two days. I would have never been able to afford it. Well, maybe I could have afforded it, but when I am on the road for ten days in a foreign land, I do not want to afford everything. I would rather keep as much spare change as possible in case of an emergency.

I was off and going to meet Bryan near Piccadilly at 11:30 a.m. I caught the tube and sat out on the street and people-watched. I noticed his familiar face emerge from the subway station. From there I followed him up to his hotel and dropped off my backpack.

We had about four hours until we needed to catch a train to the airport. To kill this time we decided to do a London pub-crawl. We ran into a girl from Argentina along the way, and she joined us on our bar hop.

It was now 3:30 p.m. and Bryan and I are back at the hotel with our bags. His mom, grandma, and sister are nowhere to be found. The taxi that is taking us to the station is waiting out front. We wait until 4:00 p.m. and finally get into the cab. From there we make our way to the station. We take a train ride for what seems like forever and finally arrive at the airport with moments to spare.

As soon as we get to the airport counter the attendant informs us that our flight is closed. This was a real bummer, and that means that we missed meeting up with the Hungarians in Paris tonight. Hopefully they will forgive us.

Our new flight leaves at 13 hours from now at 6:00 a.m. Bryan's family opted to spend 100 pounds on an airport hotel room. Bryan and I made friends with more Australians who were staying overnight in the airport. We set up camp in the airport. We are playing cards, smoking cigarettes, and exchanging stories about our travel.

I spent a world-record amount of money on a pack of Camels at the airport kiosk. They were 9 British pounds for one pack. One pound is worth roughly $2 so it cost nearly $18 for this pack. I think we will get our money's worth because between the four of us they probably will not last much longer.

24th October, 2004
11:00 a.m.

We arrived in Paris this morning. I am pretty sure Bryan's family has a bit of a chip on their shoulder about me being on the same flight. I suspect that back in the hotel room last night they privately placed the blame for the missed flight on me. I walked with them to their hotel, and Bryan wanted to take a nap.

I dropped off my bag in his room, and I am off exploring Paris. Right now, I am sitting by the Seine in Paris. I have just walked over and snapped a few pictures of the Eiffel Tower. I am going back to get my bag in a few minutes. Then I will check into my room, on the other side of Paris. Also Maxime is going to meet up with Bryan and me this afternoon and give us a Frenchman's tour of Paris. It is always nice to have someone local show me around. We fly out for Rome tomorrow morning.

25th October, 2004
11:00 a.m.

Yesterday in Paris, we met up with Max. He gave us an awesome tour of the city. We bought a few bottles of wine, stuffed them in our backpacks, and went from place to place. He even showed us a hillside in Paris where we could see the entire city.

There were painters on the street, and I asked one of the lady painters if she would paint me nude. She said she would love to, but it was windy and cold. She told me to beware she would not embellish. I decided to skip it. We walked down the street that the Moulin Rouge is on. We walked past the Moulin Rouge and stopped to take a picture from a better angle.

While we were stopped and snapping photos, a seedy gentleman came out of a door. He asked us if we wanted to come into his club. He said for five euros we could have a whiskey and Coke and watch the show from his lady performers. He said it was nothing like American clubs. His promise was that just with the cover everything was included; even the whiskey and Coke was worth five euros anywhere in Europe, so we went in.

We went inside and sat in theater style seating. Three ladies brought us our whiskey and Cokes and quickly tried to separate us. I told the one who was chatting with me to sit down. Bryan and Max stayed in their seats too. My server began telling me that I could go to the back and do whatever I wanted with her. I told her I would rather sit out here with my friends and watch whatever show was about to happen. Then I started to ask her about her family, and if she had any brothers and sisters. She and the other servers quickly got frustrated with their inability to rip us off and went back to a back room by themselves.

We told Max, who is a native Frenchman, to go ask the doorman about the show he promised. He went and asked the bouncer in French. Shortly after, the curtain opened. A girl walked out fully clothed and sat on a stool with a table in front of it. The table contained a McDonald's Value Meal that another dancer had just brought in. Our show was nothing like the Moulin Rouge-type performance we expected. It consisted of a girl on a stool, taking off articles of clothing one by one, and simultaneously eating her cheeseburger and fries. The only time she would stand up was to remove a more difficult piece of clothes. Then she immediately sat down and kept eating. We left before she got to the bottom of her super-sized freedom fries.

After this we went and sat in the park and had wine while watching the river flow by. I heard the sound of whizzing roller blades. All of a sudden there were three Paris city cops surrounding us on our bench. Max took the lead yet again and talked to them in French. Just as soon as they rolled up, they rolled away. Max said we needed to leave.

We packed our belongings and walked. I asked Max what the deal was. He said that there was no drinking allowed in the park. He told the cop he was showing his American friends around Paris, and he was not aware of the rules. The cop probably did not buy this story because there was a large sign directly behind our bench that said no alcoholic beverages were allowed. Paris was a blast. I said goodbye to Bryan and Max yesterday evening.

    I just got into Rome with Ben, his brother Jason, and his aunt. We caught another early flight, then we took a taxi to the Vatican. Ben and his family were staying at a Best Western close to the Vatican. I was looking for a somewhat different experience. I found a hostel, Colours, in the guidebook that was close to Rome's attractions. This is where I am now. I just took a shower on a rooftop tile shower overlooking the city. I have my own kitchen, and I am sharing a room with two girls from Colorado. We are about to go exploring.

26th October, 2004
11:30 p.m.

    Well, yesterday I toured the Vatican, Spanish Steps, and many other places in town. Then the girls from Colorado and I went to the grocery store and picked up groceries to make dinner. We made vegetables and pasta and had wine on the rooftop terrace.

    They have been in Rome for a few days. Our plan for tonight is to go to an American-owned bar called the Drunken Ship. They feature beer pong, flip cup, and ice-cold beer. I partook of all three, however, I am pretty sure I got hustled. The losing team bought the pitcher for the next game. The girls playing flip cup and beer pong looked like pushovers, but they were not. I must have bought six pitchers in a row before finally winning a match. Maybe they were just trying to get me on their level. After the party, we stopped at a Turkish food wagon. Then we headed back to our room for sleep.

Today we walked all around Rome and traversed much of the city. The more I walked around, the more I wanted to be out of the city. As a country boy from Dandridge, Tennessee I had grown weary of the hustle and bustle of London, Paris, and Rome. I want to spend my final days of fall break somewhere other than a city. When we get done exploring I am going to Ben's hotel. I will borrow his guidebook and see if I can find a place to go. After our daylong tour of Rome, Ben loaned me his guidebook. I informed Ben that I was going to split from them for the remainder of the trip and meet him at the airport in Venice on Sunday morning.

Then I went back to the hostel where the Colorado girls had met a gentleman from Ohio who was in Italy studying their cuisine. He was a chef, and he and friends on the next floor up wanted to put our money together and have him cook dinner for us. I pitched in my ten euros, and I went to the grocery store with the chef. We purchased 70 euros' worth of fresh bread, seafood, pork, beef, pasta, wine, sauces, and anything else the chef needed. He cooked up our meal, and it was delightful. Then for dessert I sampled Grappa. Grappa is alcohol made from grapes that is similar to moonshine in strength and taste.

I also had planning to do. Where was I going to go? I looked through the guidebook and settled on Elba Island. I would need to take a bus in the morning to Rome's central train station, then a train to Piombino followed by a ferry to the island. It looked interesting enough, so I wrote down the information on a sheet of paper and settled in with my plan.

I bid farewell to my dinner group, and I told the Colorado girls goodbye. I would be up and away before they awoke. They were in early tonight, too. All of us needed extra rest today after our good times at the Drunken Ship last night.

27th October, 2004
10:45 p.m.

I woke up early today and left the Colorado girls a farewell note. I took a train ride from Rome to Piombino and then hopped on a rather large ferry for a ride across the Mediterranean to a place I have only seen on a black-and-white book page less than twenty-four hours ago.

I arrived at Elba Island around 4:00 p.m. today and went to the tourist office. I asked them about low-cost accommodations. They sent me to the Hotel Nobel right off the main strip of the island. The cost per night was 25 euros. I settled in for three nights. I took a walk down to the harbor tonight and looked at boats. I truly enjoyed the peace and quiet. I plan to wake up early tomorrow and take pictures at sunrise, rent a moped, and work on my train schedule for getting to Venice on Sunday for my early-morning flight.

28th October, 2004
11:17 p.m.

This morning I woke up at 5:45 a.m. I was fully refreshed. I walked around the entire island taking pictures of the sunrise and the angry gray clouds as they rolled across the sea. I took a multitude of photos of the most beautiful beach settings I have ever seen. My words cannot do justice to what I experienced on this morning walk.

Then I went and toured the home that Napoleon Bonaparte was exiled to after he tried to take over the world. I witnessed his amazing ocean view, his bed, his garden, and also read about his history. Elba Island would be a great choice to serve out the remainder of my years should I ever be exiled and have a choice of destinations.

Next, I rented a scooter from a shop downtown for 25 euros and traversed every single road on the entire island in less than four hours. For a snack I grabbed pizza at a downtown pizzeria and then went by the tourist office for assistance with booking my train ticket back to Venice on Sunday. The tourist office attendant told me I had an 8-hour train ride so I would actually need to leave on Saturday. It was a good thing I woke up so early today and got everything taken care of. I still had one more full day.

I went by the grocery store and picked up snacks and walked back to my room for a shower and rest. I awoke around 8:30 p.m. and went down to a local ice cream parlor and beverage shop. I drank a few beers while watching Italian sitcoms and listening to people play foosball and presumably talk about their days. Now, I am back at the room about to retire. I plan to spend my day tomorrow sitting on the beach and relaxing.

29th October, 2004
12:47 a.m.

Today I spent most of the day taking it easy. This is something that would have not been possible if I had toured Venice and Florence. I am glad I took myself out of my comfort zone to travel alone for a bit. It really is a nice way to travel. There is only one person that needs to be pleased, myself.

I spent the entire day today without speaking one word of English. It was 8:45 p.m. I was ready to call my Elba Trip over. I walked back to my hotel to go to bed. I needed to get my gear ready to catch the Ferry back to the mainland at 8:30 a.m. for a full day of travel.

I retired back to my hotel and was walking across the hallway, when I heard footsteps coming up the stairs behind me. I turned around and a girl about my age entered the hallway. I said hello. I asked her if she spoke English. She did, and she told me she was from Switzerland. I told her that I was from America. I also mentioned that I had a bottle of wine I could not travel with tomorrow. I then asked if she would help me drink it. She said she was leaving tomorrow too. She needed to pack, but she told me to stop back by in thirty minutes and bring the wine.

She shut her hotel room door, and I ran down the stairs and across the street to the grocery store and bought a bottle of wine. I took the wine to my room and put it in my travel bag along with two cups and a wine opener. I also packed up the rest of my gear except for what I would wear on the train tomorrow.

I walked out of my room and down the hall. I pecked on her door with my knuckles. When she opened it, I told her we could easily sit here in the cheap hotel rooms and drink the wine or we could go enjoy it on the beach. After all, that is why we both came to Elba. I knew there was not much ocean front in Switzerland, and she quickly agreed. We walked down the stairs and through the roads of Elba Island to a beach access that I had first spotted around 6:00 a.m. two days before.

We sat on the wooden stairs of a beach access and talked about different subjects. She was a nurse from Switzerland who dealt with the mentally handicapped. I told her we had a lot in common, because I lived in a mental institute in the Netherlands. The look on her face was priceless. I had to follow it up quickly by telling her that I was a student, and Watersley was what they offered us for housing. She said that she came to Elba Island every fall for a week of relaxation. I could easily see why after the fantastic three days I just spent here.

30th, October, 2004
8:15 p.m.

Oh what a day. I woke up early and made my way to the Ferry to get back to Piombino. I got on the ferry and sat down. Half way across the Mediterranean a fight broke out between passengers. The brawl got so large the captain had to come down from the ships helm and place the participants under arrest.

This was all very interesting until I considered my tight travel schedule. I had to catch a bus to the train station, and my train was leaving within six minutes of the ferry's arrival on shore. I would surely miss the bus. Then I would miss my train connections later. It could be a disaster ending with me being stuck in the middle of Tuscany after missing multiple trains and flights.

The ferry finally landed fifteen minutes late. I had missed the first bus to the train station. I sat on a concrete pillar waiting for the next one. When the next bus arrived I boarded. I sat down only to see a couple thousand ants crawling on my leg. I thought they were on the bus seat. I stood up to brush them off. The people behind me were screaming, yelling, and pointing at me. I had sat in a piece of gum on the concrete pillar. I truly had ants in my pants. I ran off the bus and brushed the little bastards off of my cargo shorts before getting back on the bus and heading towards the train station.

When the bus arrived at the station there was a train stopped with the doors open. I blasted down the center aisle of the bus with no regards for anyone else and jumped onto the train without even checking where it was going or validating my ticket. It took another hour to find out I was on the correct train, going in the right direction.

    The train stopped in Florence where I was set up to catch a high-speed train to Venice, then a bus to the airport. I took my moment in Florence to grab a cheeseburger at McDonald's. The girl at the checkout noticed my accent and smiled. My two cheeseburgers magically turned into three when I opened my paper sack while waiting for the train.

    This train was delayed about an hour. Once it arrived, I boarded. The experience on this train was more like a flight. I had an assigned seat. An attendant routinely checked if I needed a beverage or snack. When the train arrived I got on with my backpack and settled in.

    I arrived in Venice about an hour ago. I checked the bus schedule so that I could find the airport. I am not sure what hotel Ben is staying at tonight so I was going to see if there were any hotels close to the airport's bus stop. Our flight leaves around 6:30 a.m. I feel a need to have my lodging as close as possible to the airport. I got off the bus at airport, and there were no hotels. I made the decision to grab a bite to eat and see what happens. Now I am sitting at the airport, and getting tired. I may just wait here until the morning flight.

31st, October, 2004
4:12 a.m.

    I woke up about twenty minutes ago and the airport was pitch black. Apparently, this is not an airport that stays open all night. After getting my bearings, I begin realizing I was the only one left in the entire airport. I got up and walked to the bathroom to brush my teeth and wash my face. I arrived back to my seat and was eating trail mix. I noticed two military Jeeps pull up under the front entry canopy of the airport. Instantly, fifteen special operations soldiers armed with handguns, M-16's, and laser sighted assault rifles came busting through the entrance yelling at me in Italian. I instinctively put my hands up in the air.

    The Italian soldiers made me slide them my passport across the floor while I was face down on the cold airport floor. As I lay there on the ground, I could see the weapon's red lasers of death dancing all over the floor surrounding my head and face. After seeing my passport was from the United States, one of the soldiers started speaking to me in English.

    "What the hell are you doing here?" The soldier yelled inquisitively.

    "I have an early flight the next morning, and I must have fallen asleep. I was not aware airports in Italy were not open all night." I told him in slow intentional English.

    "This is not a hotel." He snapped back at me. Then he handed me my passport back and here I sit.

31st October, 2004
6:12 a.m.

    I am still sitting here at the airport checked into my flight. Ben is nowhere to be found. I do not know if he switched up his flight or if something happened to him. Our flight leaves in eighteen minutes so he will need to get a move on. My trip started with missing a flight in London. I am sure as Hell not going to miss another one in Venice.

31st October, 2004
6:12 a.m.

    Ben showed up finally. I know the time on this post shows the exact same time as the previous post. Well, last night was Daylight Saving Time. Apparently, they practice this ritual in Italy too. I had to wait an extra hour here at the airport. Ben was privy to this information. He showed up about fifteen minutes ago. We are about to board our flight to Brussels.

31st October, 2004
4:15 p.m.

    I am almost home and catching our final connection in Maastricht, to Sittard. The flight from Venice to Brussels went directly over the Alps. It was very turbulent. Everyone on the flight had to feel like this was the worst flight ever. The plane shook the entire time. When we touched down, all the passengers erupted in a round of applause. It was that scary. We then caught a train from Brussels to Liege'.

I had to use the bathroom while waiting at Liege' station, for our connection. I went into the bathroom. They had a man collecting money to use the bathroom. I bypassed him and used the bathroom. Then I walked right by him on the way out. Through my peripheral vision I could see that he was giving chase. I doubled back like Jason Bourne, and hid behind a kiosk. He ran by me. I went up another ramp and found Ben standing on the platform. I told him what happened. About that time, the bathroom manager grabbed my arm from behind. I told him I did not have any money and to buzz off. He did.

The one bad thing about losing weight and developing six pack abs is that I no longer have room in my abdomen to hold urine. I have to go to the bathroom every 30 minutes. This is rather costly, because in Europe there is a charge to use a public restroom. In Tennessee, this practice is illegal.

1st November, 2004
1:30 p.m.

Back to class and just had neon green split pea soup and bread. I really missed it during my week off. It is amazing talking to the students from Europe and realizing that most of them had never seen as many countries and cities in Europe over their entire life. Here I am seeing the world at an incredible pace.

I spoke to Bryan last night. We are going to plan a trip to Prague in December. He had a nice fall break. His family made it home to St. Louis without any issues.

2nd November, 2004
1:30p.m.

Today is Election Day, in the United States. I have mailed my absentee ballot in three weeks ago. It is astonishing how interested all of my other classmates are in our election. It is also amazing how much the people in Europe hate George W. Bush. I do not think it is the fact that they like John Kerry, as much as they just do not like George Bush. I think, for them, he is just a popular person to dislike. This is mainly because of wars in Iraq and Afghanistan. A large portion of Europe does not support these campaigns.

I love my country, and I support our president whether they are a Democrat or a Republican. If anyone gives me grief about the United States or George W. Bush I can turn the tables on him or her rather quickly. First, I ask them when is the next election in their home country? Next, I question them about who is running? Then, I follow up with asking them if they voted in their last election? Amazingly enough, Europeans are extremely interested in our election, thousands of miles away. I have rarely found someone my age that actually takes the time to cast a ballot in their own election and flex their own democratic freedoms. I mailed my vote in from thousands of miles away. checkmate Europe.

4th November 2004
Letter from home:

To: Dearest Son Jobe
From: Your Loving Mother

Hi Honey,

    I have been meaning to write all week. I want to make sure you get this letter before Thanksgiving. We will surely miss you at our table son. Our thoughts will be with you and we shall toast to your health and your smiling face. Today was the Night of the Patriots for the student body. It was pretty good. Not as good as when you and Peggy used to be in them, but entertaining.
    Your little sister Kim came home last night to buy her Delta Gamma little sister, Allison Cole, goodies at the Campus Cargo Store in Dandridge. She has to go back today for a 2:00 p.m. class. They have initiation this weekend so she probably will not be back until Thanksgiving time.
    Your sister Peggy went to Philadelphia yesterday for a nursing conference. The University of Tennessee sent ten student nurses and paid their expenses. I am glad she got to go. Her tonsils are still bothering her. They will come out after Christmas. It's already planned and scheduled.
    Dad is doing well. Seems to like his new job real well. Not stressed out all the time. I'm sure it will add years on to his life. We planned to go up to the cabin tonight for the weekend (it's Friday here today). Poco is fine and so is Jamocha. She slept with Kim last night and they always go to the cabin with us

and get lots of attention. They love going. We load them up in the back seat just like "kid-dogs." They know exactly where they are going too. It is almost like Poco can tell when it is Friday because she is ready to jump in the car as soon as I get home on Fridays.

Aunt Bert and Uncle Ray will not be coming for Thanksgiving they are having their kids to their house this year. We are probably going to go to the mountain for Thanksgiving. Tomorrow morning Jim is coming to help your Dad put in propane logs in the basement fireplace. It will warm up the downstairs, fast! I hope it does.

I am going to see Dr. Greg Sexton at 4:00 p.m. Monday for a cavity filling. I will tell him to put the Nitrous up high as it goes. I hate those shots in the gums, don't you? Our new Mayor is George Gantee, my friend Betty's son. I am so thrilled that he won.

Well honey bunny, it is going to get busy here. I need to get tests ready for my students. I hope your school is going good and that you are learning your Dutch. Say your prayers and remember how much Daddy and I love you.

Our Love,

Mom & Dad

10th November, 2004
3:45 p.m.

I just got back from class and getting groceries, and I have very sad news to report. One of the Hungarian girls, Eszter, is very sick. I spoke with her roommates today, and I asked them where she was. They told me that she was at the doctor, and she was ill. They explained it to me the best they could in English.

It seems Eszter has a disease called Tony Salitus. I am under the impression that this must be similar to Lou Gerig's disease. Typically if a disease is bad enough to be named after someone, it is pretty bad. I asked the girls what it affected and they pointed to the upper body and portions of the head and torso. They did not know all the specifics.

I am a bit concerned for myself too. I might have stolen a kiss or two from her over the past two weeks. The anxiety of not knowing exactly what Tony Salitus is or how it spreads is nerve racking.

12th November, 2004
2:55 p.m.

I am back at Watersley having a bit of a chuckle as I write this. Eszter was back in class today and recovering from her illness. She was doing much better. It seems that Tony Salitus is not a disease named after someone, after all. It is actually tonsillitis and this is the way it sounds when a

Hungarian pronounces the syllables. Toni-sill-it-is... Tony Salitus.

I am glad she is well. All my anxiety was for nothing. Judging by my Mother's letters, I guess my sister back home in Tennessee is suffering from Tony Salitus too. It must be going around.

16th November, 2004
5:25 a.m.

Right now I am sitting at the Amsterdam train station. Last night around 9:30, I went down to Bryan's room to play chess. Sometime during our first game we decided we would go to Amsterdam. We are about a 2-hour train ride to Amsterdam from Sittard and the last train leaves around 11:00 p.m. Our plan was to enjoy the nightlife there until the clubs close and then catch the first train back in the morning, which leaves at 5:30 a.m. We would then arrive back for our 9:30 a.m. classes.

While playing chess we heard the French people who live in our building talking. We asked them if they wanted to go. We now have five people on our journey. I called over to the Hungarian's house to see if they wanted to go. Brett and the Hungarian girls cannot make it, but Max wants to go. We tell him to meet us at the train station in an hour.

We enjoyed Golden Showers and beers on the train ride to Amsterdam and arrive there around midnight. We went from bars to clubs until everything was closed. It was around 3:30 a.m. We walked towards the train station. It is as quiet as anyone will ever see

Amsterdam Central station. We purchased our ticket for the first train back and sat on the loading platform benches.

    Every fifteen minutes, an Amsterdam city policeman comes over and raps his nightstick against our bench. It is not illegal to wait on a train, but it is illegal to sleep at the station. He would like to remind us to stay awake. This has gone on for the past two hours. Only five minutes, and finally we get to board our train and head back home.

19th November, 2004
11:00 a.m.

    Today as soon as Ben and I get out of our External Reporting Accounting class we are going to Germany. Last year there were two German tennis players, Chris and Dominik. They both played tennis for Tennessee Tech. My friend at Tennessee Tech, Will Chappell, also played tennis for the university. He introduced us. After the school year, they moved back to Germany. Ben kept in touch. They invited us to Stuttgart for the weekend. It is about seven-hour train ride to get there. We should have a really good time.

20th November, 2004
1:00 p.m.

    When we arrived in Stuttgart, Chris and Dominik met us at the train station. They greeted us with smiles and forty ounces of German beer in a gangster style brown paper bag. We toasted to meeting again and went to the front of the central station to get on a bus. We boarded the bus, and I watched out the window as we went through the streets of Stuttgart. We got off at their apartment and went upstairs to drop off our bags. After setting down our gear, we hopped on another bus and rode to another train station. From there we went to the Porsche factory, museum, and showroom. What an impressive factory. There were many different types of models they offer in Germany compared to the half of dozen choices I would have had in the United States.

    After we were done touring Porsche, we went to a Christmas market and drank gluhwine. This drink is a mix of red wine, cloves, orange peels, and cinnamon. Gluhwine is served piping hot in a rented coffee mug. I put a deposit on my mug, and I got the money back when it was returned. While walking around the Christmas market there were pastries for sale, ice-skating, and many festivities celebrating the season. This is the norm for most German towns this time of year. Chris and Dominik tell us that tonight we are going to their university for a party. We finish our gluhwine and head back to the apartment to get ready. I literally had not stopped drinking since they handed me the bottled beer when we got off the train. I am very tired.

    We arrived at the university around midnight. This was a raucous party. The building it is held in is the university center. It is a humongous building much like the university center at any American university. On weekends, once a month, the university hosts a party for the students. On one end of the building, there is a live band. On the other end, there is a D.J. Both the band and D.J. are playing extremely loud music. I would estimate that 1,500 students were in the building's middle corridor.

There are several bars, staffed by university employees. I can get a beer for around two euros. In addition, I pay four euros as a deposit for my first beer. This guarantees that I will bring the bottle back to them. As opposed to smashing it on the floor or over someone's head and losing my deposit. We all grab beer and sit down at an indoor table.

The next thing I know, I am being carried out the front door by university security guards. Apparently, while Ben and the Germans went to get a refill I fell asleep on the picnic table in the university center. They were pushing me out the door and locking it just as Ben ran up and said something to them. The door unlocked and the security guards opened it. I promised them I would not fall back asleep and walked back inside to rejoin the party.

Now it is Ben and the Germans who are getting tired. I feel obligated to keep up my promise to not fall asleep. I am out on the D.J.'s dance floor breaking out some bitching dance moves. I start dancing with a dark eyed German girl. We must have danced for an hour before Ben comes over and tells me it is time go. For some reason I just flagged him away and kept dancing. It was now an hour later and 3:00 a.m. I am sitting at the table I fell asleep on two hours ago talking to the German girl I danced with.

Apparently, Ben, Chris, and Dominik left me at a strange German University. I am in a town that I have only been in for less than twelve hours. For some reason I do not care. The dancing partner asks me if I want to join her and her friends for a Turkish kabob and a drink at a late nightclub across town.

It is about 4:00 a.m. I am sitting on a couch in a late nightclub somewhere in Germany. I do not remember the name or location. The girl I danced with is now sitting on my lap in a dark, laser lit, German after hours club. We are holding hands and making out in public, with as much class as possible. I really should be more careful about contracting Tony Salitus.

At 5:00 a.m. the club closed. A bouncer shuffled us out the door. I walk down the street with her to the train station. The first train of the morning arrives at 5:30 a.m. I am still kissing her while the hydraulic door opens. She hops on the train and the door closes. She waves goodbye from the window as the train begins to move. I run alongside the train chasing it and wiping imaginary tears from my eyes until the platform ends. Then the train moves slowly out of sight.

I am now somewhere in Stuttgart, Germany. It is sunrise. I have no clue where Chris, Dominik, or Ben is. My first guess is at their apartment, in bed. I buy a train ticket to Stuttgart Central station and begin to retrace my steps from earlier that day.

After getting off at the train station in Stuttgart, I go to the front of the station where the busses pick up. I try to remember which bus we had rode earlier. I cannot recall the number off the top of my head. I watch as bus after bus passes by hoping something will trip my memory.

I take a chance on a bus that seems familiar. I am not positive about its destination. I ride through the streets of Stuttgart at 6:15 A.M looking out the window hoping something will look familiar. I notice something that looks recognizable and run up the aisle to get off the bus. Once I get off, I realize I am at the wrong stop. I can still see the bus in the distance, and I watch its route until it goes out of sight.

Now I am hiking through the streets at 6:45 a.m. I am in an unfamiliar town with no regard to whether this is the ghetto or a high crime area. I am completely oblivious. I have walked in the busses direction as far as I could see it go. I then find another bus stop. I look across the street and there is Chris and Dominik's apartment. I walk over to the lobby door. It is locked. The German's apartment was on the 4th floor of the building from what I remembered. So, I began throwing small to medium sized pebbles at their window.

It is now around 7:30 a.m. The pebbles did not work. A lady came out of the door. I tried to go in while she left it open. She would not let me in, and I almost got pepper sprayed. Then the newspaper delivery guy came to drop off the morning paper around 8:15 a.m. I tried the same maneuver with him. He blocked me out as well, and I tried to explain my situation in English. He said that he could not let me in. Then he pointed to a doorbell on the exterior wall with all the tenants' names on it. There was a private intercom for each apartment that I had overlooked.

I scrolled down the names and found my friend's apartment. I gave their room number a buzz. There was no answer. I gave the button a longer buzz. Still no answer, and I wondered if I was ringing the correct apartment.

"Hallo?" The intercom spoke to me.

I said, "It is me, Jobe."

"Jobe? We thought we would never see you again!" The intercom rang back.

Moments later the entry door opened. I walked up four flights of stairs and got in bed around 8:45 a.m.

21st November, 2004
3:42 p.m.

We are almost back to Sittard from Stuttgart. Yesterday, after sleeping off the night before, we went to Munich and went sight seeing. We finished off the day by ordering pizza and calling it an early night.

My train ticket on the way here was 90 euros. Dominik has a student identification card that gives him 75% off train tickets in Germany. The plan was to use it to buy my ticket. I would mail the identification card back to him. I would be in major trouble if my ticket was checked, and the ID was proven to not be mine. I would go to jail and be deported. I was an illegal alien anywhere in the European Union, including Germany.

We told Chris and Dominik goodbye and thanks. Then we boarded our train back to Sittard. I sat down and put on a headband and sunglasses. Then I hoped for the best. When I got my ticket checked the attendant did not say anything to me. I was armed with minimal German phrases. If the conductor had asked me anything in depth, my cover would have been blown.

23rd November, 2004
Greeting card from home:

"Thanksgiving is – a gathering of family and friends, a harvest of memories and sharing, a bounty of caring and love."

Hi Honey,

What do the Dutch do for Thanksgiving? Anything? Is it just an American holiday? We miss you, and we will see you in a month, be good, or as good as you can be.

    Love you,

    Mom, Dad, Peggy, Kim, Poco, Jamocha, Bubba, Lil Kitty.

November 24th, 2004
3:30 p.m.

    Class is done for this week and tomorrow is Thanksgiving. They have given the entire school the day off for some other holiday not named Thanksgiving. I have been in limbo for the past month as to what we will do. We had initially planned to go to Maastricht. Sue, the bartender at the Shamrock, promised us turkey, dressing, and all the fixings. Then we could watch NFL football on the big screen at the Irish pub. For some reason, I feel like I want to share the Thanksgiving experience with my classmates. I am beginning to put together some recipes right now and a grocery list.

**25th November, 2004
5:45 p.m.**

This morning I woke up bright and early and rode to the grocery store on my bike. I had recipes for scratch mash potatoes, green bean casserole, gravy, homemade stuffing, turkey, and a honey glazed ham. I got to the store and found all the items I needed except for one thing, turkey.
 I asked the butcher, and described the bird using gobble noises and hand jestures. We decided what I was looking for was the Dutch equivalent of kalkoen. I imagined they named it this because of the sound a turkey makes, but I am really not sure.
 The butcher looked around his meat department saying, "Kalkoen, hmmm?, kalkoen, ahhhhh, kalkoen, ummmm?"
 He did this for almost five minutes, while I walked behind him. Finally, he pushed aside a large side of pork in the cooler and there it was, a package of turkey. The only turkey in the store, and it was not a full American style bird, but more like lunchmeat. It was thinly sliced and packaged in a zip bag. It would have to do. I was not going to be the American who cooked Thanksgiving for the Europeans and did not have turkey on the menu.

I rode my bike over to the Hungarian's house. This is where I had decided to cook the feast. I had three bags of groceries hanging off each handle bar. The ride was so unstable I could just see myself falling over with all the bags spilling on the roadside. I made it safely to their place, and it was now around 10:30 a.m. Everyone was just getting out of bed. Brett let me in. I told him my plan.

We began going through the recipes and preparing the feast. We mashed up over 15 lbs of potatoes, made a whole loaf of bread into fresh stuffing, and made two full pans of green been casserole with crisp onions on top. For the ham we sliced it in lunchmeat slices just like the turkey. Then we loaded the middle of the turkey and ham with mashed potatoes, gravy, and stuffing then rolled them like burritos. After this we placed them on a cookie sheet and baked them to perfection with a slight honey glaze on top.

Around 2:45 p.m. the house smelled delightful with all the Thanksgiving delicacies. Our group had grown to Ben, the Hungarians, the French, the Finnish, and several Dutch students from our class. Before we served the meal I asked everyone to go around the room and tell what they were thankful for. It was truly a Thanksgiving to remember. I plan to call my family tonight to tell them how much I miss and love them.

30th November, 2004
1:30 a.m.

The one thing we did not have on Thanksgiving was football. We decided to go to Maastricht tonight to watch. Bryan had his friend Caroline in town. I had dinner with her in Rotterdam a month or so before. She has a car so she offered to drive us to Maastricht. This way we can watch a full game instead of having to leave in the fourth quarter, because the last train is leaving.

This was only the third time I had ridden in a car over the past three months. Most days in the United States I ride in a car at least three times per day. It is almost humorous how Bryan and I speak of girls we meet with cars. It reminds me of the the Summer Nights song from the movie Grease.

"Like did she have a car?"
"Uh-huh, uh-huh, uh-huh, uh huh."

2nd December, 2004
2:00 p.m.

Just finished up a group meeting here at school and had a nice bowl of soup and bread. Bryan and I leave for Dortmund tomorrow. Then we will fly out to Prague on Friday morning. Ben is already in the Czech Republic. We will meet up with him in Prague.

4th December, 2004
8:00 a.m.

I am sitting at the Dortmund airport waiting to board a plane to Prague with Bryan. Last night we arrived in Dortmund by train around 10:00 p.m. We dropped our bags off at a hostel. We did not check in. Bryan knew a bartender in Dortmund. He wanted to ask him if we could crash at his place. The hostel manager said it would be acceptable to leave our bags until midnight. If we needed a room, then he would still rent us one.

We walked through Dortmund's Christmas market and stood next to the largest Christmas tree ever. It encompassed 200 trees all meshed into one. We went to a bar where Bryan's friend worked. We talked with our server for a few minutes before asking if she knew Bryan's friend. She said she did and that he was on break. The she inquisitively asked us how we knew him. Bryan told her that he was his boyfriend. This was untrue, but we never told his coworker otherwise.

Bryan's friend came off break and talked with us. His living situation was not one that would allow us to crash at his place tonight. This was ok, because we still had the hostel. We relaxed at the bar. Eventually we engaged in a conversation with another group of Germans. We told them we were going to check in at the hostel and they invited us to crash on their couches. In the morning they would take us to the airport. We took them up on the offer and grabbed our bags from the hostel. We went and slept on couches at their place.

I woke up this morning and light had shown its way on another strange place. I smelled coffee and toasted bread in the air. I stood up and walked around the corner. Our new friends had a breakfast prepared. It was toast, coffee, and boiled eggs. The table was set for us. I woke Bryan up, and we ate. Then we rode in his car to the airport. We told him thank you. Now here we sit.

**5th December, 2004
11:30 a.m.**

We arrived in Prague yesterday morning and found our way to the same hostel Ben was staying at. We checked in a room with eight beds, but it was just Bryan and I. We explored the city. It turned out that there was Elvis impersonator who worked at a bar in the city center. He told us they would have karaoke starting at 8:30 p.m. Plus they had ESPN, and Tennessee was playing Auburn in the SEC championship game tonight. I would get to watch my first Tennessee football game of the season. My only connection to the Vols this season was reading about them on the Internet.
In the meantime, we asked Elvis about other places in town that were worthwhile. He pointed on our map to an author's club near our hostel. He said it was a good atmosphere and only for locals. The door was inconspicuous. Our best bet was to just walk in like we owned the place. Bryan and I walked around town until we spotted the door.
We opened it and inside was over 100 people sitting at wooden tables and enjoying

themselves. We made our way to a two-seat table and sat down. The server came over and we had beers and began chatting.

A Czech girl at an adjoining table turned around and said, "So what are two stray Americans doing in here?"

Before I knew it Bryan and her were in a heated conversation. This ranged from world politics to the children's books she authored. We talked with her for nearly an hour and collected our tab. We both had four beers each. Our combined tab was the American equivalent of 80 cents. At ten cents per beer we decided we would stop back by tomorrow night.

It was now 5:30 in the afternoon and we went by the hostel where we met up with Ben. For dinner, we decided to go to a TGI Fridays we had spotted earlier. When we got there it was Jack Daniel's night so we drank Jack and Cokes. I had baby back ribs and French fries.

I glanced around the familiar looking franchise restaurant that was decorated with American décor. I noticed something behind a booth. I walked closer not minding the couple that was sitting at the table below it. It was a Carson Newman College pennant hanging on the wall of the TGI Fridays, in Prague. This was peculiar to me because I grew up in Dandridge, Tennessee. Carson Newman College is 10 miles away in Jefferson City. My mother was the school's nurse for several years while I was growing up.

After dinner we went back to the hotel to rest a bit before the SEC Championship game and karaoke. We met Australian girls at our hostel and invited them to join us, and they did. Once at the bar we drank beers and watched the game. As the game was going on, we started singing karaoke. Ben, Bryan, and I sang Garth Brooks, Friends In Low Places. We brought the entire bar to their feet with applause.

Then a few songs later I was called up to recite Queen's, Bohemian Rhapsody. I hit every note. The crowd went crazy. I was able to crowd surf back over to our table. I think that this was the most English these people had ever heard in their lives, and they really enjoyed it.

It was now closing time at the bar, and Tennessee had lost the football game. We collected our tabs and while paying them Elvis came over to our table. He leaned over to inform us that we had won the karaoke competition. He asked us what we would like to drink for our prize. It is hard to explain the thrill of winning a prize for something that we did not even know we entered.

We asked Elvis for rum and Coke and thought we might get a cocktail glass each to sip on. When Elvis came back he had a full nine-beer pitcher of the strongest rum and Coke I have ever tasted in my life. Bryan, Ben, the Australian girls, and I sat and talked as we polished off our first place trophy.

6th December, 2004
3:45 a.m.

Yesterday we woke up around noon and explored the city. We found the American embassy in Prague. Then we walked around the Christmas market, before heading back to the author's pub. We met the same girl there who Bryan had talked with yesterday. She took us around to the clubs in town that she thought we would like. Before we knew it, it was 3:30 a.m. We had a 9:30 a.m. flight to catch. We parted ways and went back to our hostel.

6th December, 2004
11:00 a.m.

Bryan and I awoke suddenly.
The desk clerk at the hostel said, "If you are going to stay another day you need to pay now."
Bryan mumbled, "What time is it?"
The desk nonchalantly informed us "It is 9:05."
We went from sound sleep to solid panic in five seconds. Bryan and I jumped out of bed and threw our clothes in bags. We yelled at the clerk to call us a cab. We ran to the street and a cab picked us up promptly. We told the driver we would give him the rest of our Czech money if he would drive as fast as possible to the airport so we did not miss our flight.

We arrived at the airport around 9:25 a.m. certain we had missed another flight. We went to check in, and luckily enough our plane was delayed one-hour due to mechanical issues. Thank God.

**8th December, 2004
1:32 p.m.**

This is my last week of class. It is truly time to hunker down. Last night I decided I would go to school early today. I would study for five hours until my first class started. I got up, took a shower, and made my way down to our apartment's bike garage.

When I got to my bike, I unlocked it. Then I backed it out of the steel rack. I sat down and started to peddle towards the door. The pedals were ridiculously hard to turn. The back wheel slugged along. I had a flat.

Great! The only day all semester I get up early to go to school and study. I have no way to get there. I began to devise a plan to get to school in alternative fashion. My eyes move down the row of bicycles still on the stand. First, I look for the ones that have not been moved in the longest amount of time. I then I look for the ones with the easiest locks to disengage. The signs that I have truly accepted the Dutch culture is that I know how to ride a bicycle, and I also know how to unlock a bike without a key.

Before I move a bike that is not mine, I think about the 24-hour security guard in the apartment office. His security camera is on the wall slowly panning around the bike garage. I nonchalantly place my bike back in the rack and walk upstairs to the security office. At this moment, the security guard is dosed off in his desk chair. I edge closer and take a look at his security screen from an angle while pretending to read a brochure on the front desk. The TV screen is on. It shows the camera in the bike garage. The VCR recording the scenes is switched to off, and the tape is ejected.

    I quietly place the brochure down and make my way down the stairs to the bike garage. Once there I find the bike I had spotted earlier and pull it off the rack. I pick up the back seat slightly so I can easily move the bike out the door without the rear wheel catching on the bike lock. I open the door, and find myself outside away from the camera view.

    Now, to render the lock useless, what I do is run full speed with the bike rolling only on the front wheel. When I reach an appropriate speed I place my palm behind the seat and drop the rear wheel while pushing forward on the seat. The force of the spokes against the wheel lock is enough to break the lock off. I cruised down Watersley hill after a quick brake check.

    I studied all morning and got plenty taken care of. I was now ready for my last week of class. I have been sitting in class for fifteen minutes. Celine, a French girl, comes in late and begins talking in French to her friends. She is frantic. I hear the French girls explain to the Finish girls what has happened. They speak in English this time.

    Apparently, someone had stolen her bike from Watersley's bike garage. She had to take the bus, and she was late for class. I knew right then I had to confess. As soon as there was a lull in the class, I made my way to an empty seat by Celine. I told her my story of wanting to study and having a flat on my bike. I also let her know that I did not intentionally steal her bike. I thought that her bike was one that had been abandoned.

To calm the waters I offered a new bike lock to replace the one I broke. Also I gave her a full pack of bus tickets to replace the one she used this morning to get to school. Finally, I gave her immediate rights to her bicycle so that she could ride home from class. I now have no bike once more, but it is only four days until I head home.

9th December, 2004
11:00 p.m.

Today Ben's friend Becca West and her sister were in Sittard. All three of them grew up in Sparta, Tennessee. These two sisters are taking a trip with Ben, after he finishes his finals. They visited our apartments at Watersley. Then they took us to an Italian restaurant for dinner. It is always nice to see familiar faces.

10th December, 2004
3:00 p.m.

I just finished my last final of the semester. I have to begin packing my things at Watersley. I am going to load up my two large bags on the bus and take them to the Hungarian's flat. For my last night in Sittard,

I will stay with the Eszter, Gina, Nora, Brett, and Max at Geuweg. They live close to the station. The next morning I will catch a cab to the train station, a bus to the airport, a plane to Amsterdam, then a flight to Detroit, followed by a final trip to Nashville.

11th December, 2004
7:30 p.m.

   It is a bittersweet time as this is the last of my nights in the Netherlands. I am at the Hungarian's house. The past three days have reminded me of yearbook day at Maury Middle School. I have open pages in this journal. I let each of my friends write in their signature, a message, and any contact information for future correspondence. We share final laughs, and then I go to bed.

12th December, 2004
8:30 a.m.

   I am sitting at the train station with two humongous bags overlooking Sittard's skyline. A light snow begins to fall from a foggy gray sky. This morning I awoke at 6:00 a.m. and took a shower. When I got out of the shower the Hungarians had prepared a full breakfast for me and were drinking tea and smoking cigarettes.
   The early morning conversation was typical, but the pending goodbyes weighed thick in the air. At around 7:00 a.m. my taxicab pulled up, and Nora, Gina, and Eszter began to cry. I gave them a hug and let them

know I would come visit them as soon as I could, and that we would keep in touch. I took the cab, and here I sit at the train station, ready to embark on my return journey to the United States.

5th May, 2005
1:00 p.m.

My updates have been few and far between. I was undergoing the pressure of moving back to the United States, finishing my last semester of college at Tennessee Tech, and enjoying my only semester in college when I was actually twenty one. I am one hundred percent sure I will graduate in two days with a Bachelor of Science in Business Administration.

Last night my roommates Drew, Brady, Matt, and me threw our last party of our collegiate career. We had set attendance records over the past two years at our keg parties. We had a great house two hundred yards from campus. Our past parties had seen everything from girl fights to coffee table dance offs. However, last night was the final one, and it was epic.

We typically charged around five dollars for a cup. This would provide someone with all of the keg beer they could possibly drink. Any profits were invested in additional kegs. We finished four last night. This was on the high end of what we had accomplished in the past. To make sure people did not skip out on paying we used a special cup for each party. Fittingly for this party we used purple and gold Solo cups to commemorate our graduations.

On our ride to get food today at 11:30 a.m., I could see the reach of last night's mixer. All the way from our house to campus there were tire marks in the grass. Smashed purple and gold solo cups covered on side of the road. The entire loop around our house still had cars parked on it and the garbage surrounding them was unmistakably ours.

Drew brought his girlfriend Christine, then Matt and I joined them for post party hangover pizza at Pizza Hut. We sat down at the table, and decided we were starving. To fill this hunger it was going to take at least three large pizzas, with breadsticks, and a dessert pizza. After we finished the first 1-½ pizzas, it was obvious we had ordered too much. Promptly we requested large to-go boxes, and went out the door.

It was a hot day for a hangover. We made it to Christine's car and noticed she had a flat tire. Surveying the situation, we concluded we could not change over to the spare on the steaming, hot, black asphalt. We would drive up the street 300 yards to a gas station and re-inflate the tire. We would follow that up with a can of Fix-a-Flat. We all jumped in the car and proceeded out of the parking lot.

As we were passing by the Pizza Hut entranceway, people began running outside wildly flailing their hands and chasing Christine's car. I reasoned that they were concerned about us driving on a flat tire. From the backseat, I rolled down Christine's crank style window.

"It's ok, we know!" I yelled to the seven people now chasing us.

I then waved and gave them a thumb's up, as I quickly rolled the window back up. We continued out of the parking lot. Not wanting to lose momentum on the flat tire Christine turned the car onto the freeway and into a slight break in traffic. About the time we reached the middle lane we heard a large skidding sound. We began exchanging glances inside the car. Then we noticed a shadow in the rearview mirror. I looked at the side mirrors in an effort to see what had happened.

After a tumble, a roll, and a flip our full smorgasbord of pizza, in two large boxes, landed upside down and the box opened wide in the middle of the road. The pizza was instantly ruined. We all erupted in uncontrollable laughter. We began wondering what the Pizza Hut patrons had thought when I rolled down the window and told them we knew. We thought they were informing us that we had a flat tire. In reality, they were trying to let us know we left our pizzas were on top of the car.

11th August, 2006
11:00 a.m.

I have now been out of school and in the U.S. workforce for over a year now. Today is the day that I will move out of my parents' place. It was very humbling moving in with my parents for a year after being on my own at college for the last four years. I really appreciate everything my parents have done for me. In return, I was able to help them mow the yard and with household chores.

I have held the same job, with Hearthstone Homes, for over a year. I started studying for my M.B.A. at Lincoln Memorial University this spring. I am taking the maximum number of hours each semester, including the summer. I will finish by next May if I keep up the same hasty pace. My bank account has swelled to over $25,000 while making a big boy paycheck and not having to pay rent. With this money I have been able to pay for my entire MBA with cash. I now have the confidence to fully launch to my own apartment after about 14 months of living back home.

7th May, 2007
1:32 p.m.

Two days ago I graduated with my MBA from Lincoln Memorial. I started classes in the spring of 2006 and finished in about a year and a half. I took full loads each semester and summer school. I also worked full time. For my graduation present, I have just booked a trip to Hungary to visit Eszter, Nora, and Gina. They live in Budapest, Hungary. I spoke to Max in France yesterday. He is also going to join us.

1st August, 2007
6:30 a.m.

My bags are packed and it is now time for my graduation present to myself. I board a plane today in Knoxville. Then I go from there to Atlanta. Once in Atlanta, I will fly to Paris. Then I am finally off to Budapest. I have not taken a long flight like this in three years. The anxiety is building. I am not as nervous as the first time I took a flight across the ocean.

2nd August, 2007
4:30 p.m.

I arrived in Budapest about an hour ago. Nora, Gina, and Eszter greeted me at the airport. We had beer and coffee at an airport café while we waited on Maxime to arrive. He was flying in from France too. About 45 minutes later we spotted him walking off the tarmac. We all went to greet him. It seemed recent, but it had already been three years since I was saying goodbye to them at their home off of Geuweg in the Netherlands. We now had a 10-day reunion in Budapest.

3rd August, 2007
4:00 a.m.

I am about to go to bed. I am certain I will not get jet lag this time. I blasted through the evening and stayed up with my friends. We played cards and told stories. Then we sampled wine and Jagermeister.

Right now it is 9:00 p.m. in the United States. This is the normal bedtime for me.

The Hungarian girls have a full week planned out. We plan to explore museums, the Hungarian countryside, a music festival, and plenty of nightlife. They arranged for us to be picked up at the airport in a Mercedes van and even after three years of being apart they still treat me like royalty.

Their apartment is centrally located on a street in Budapest. There is a trolley system that passes right by their door. Best of all, there is a Pizza Hut right underneath their building of flats. With no car I should be in no danger of leaving my leftovers on top of anything.

4th August, 2007
11:30 p.m.

Today we toured a park and rented bicycles to ride around on. It sparked nostalgia as we cycled. Then we ran around the park barefooted and tossed Frisbee to each other. One downside of the trip is that my allergies are really bothering me. My nose has been running the entire time and my voice is nasally. My sneezing, sniffing, and other symptoms have to be annoying my hosts. I am not sure what to do other than carry napkins with me everywhere I go.

5th August, 2007
3:23 a.m.

Tonight we went to a large shopping mall called the Mammout. Inside the mall they had a club. We danced to 80's music and had an experience similar to De Buren, in Sittard. Tomorrow we are going to stay at Gina's boyfriend's house in Budapest. We are currently at Nora's apartment, but her mother is not keen on her having boys staying at her place. Eszter is certain she will do a surprise apartment inspection. The Hungarian girls are going to stow Max and I across town for a day while Nora's mom is nearby.

6th August, 2007
11:23 p.m.

We played poker tonight with Gina's boyfriend and some of his friends. They like playing Texas hold'em. In each hand I played they gave me quite a good beating. My bets were risky, considering I was not playing with real money. Now I am lying on the couch about to go to sleep. Tomorrow we will tour a castle with Eszter.

7th August, 2007
8:35 p.m.

I rode around on a paddleboat with Eszter and Max around a ancient castle's moat. Next, we took a long walk around the city and by the sides of the river. Tomorrow, Max will fly back to Paris, and Eszter and I plan to attend the Sziget festival. It is one of the largest musical festivals in Europe. I imagine it is similar to Bonnaroo. We are going to watch Pink and The Chemical Brothers show. There is also a local band that Eszter knows some of the members. We bought our day passes for the festival this afternoon.

For dinner tonight I made everyone hamburgers and French-fries. I made ½ lb burger patties and fresh cut fries. No one else appreciated the large patties and only ate a portion of their red meat feast. I will have something to snack on when we get back from dancing around 3:30 a.m.

One of the many great things about this trip is I have not had to get off of my American time schedule. I go to bed at 4:00 a.m. This is 9:00 p.m. in the United States. Then I wake up at Noon, which is 6:00 a.m. at home. Then we do it all over again.

9th August, 2007
4:15 a.m.

Today we told Max goodbye and dropped him off at the Budapest airport. We came back to Nora's apartment and took a nap before we got ready to go the festival. Once at the festival it was madness. It is unnerving enough at a music event like Bonnaroo, with one hundred thousand people from all over Europe, speaking different languages.

There were downright scary moments. Eszter and I weaved through the crowds with the only thing connecting us being a hand or a grasped shirt tail. If I got lost during one turn it might be next year before they finally found me. I only speak about three words of Hungarian. They all deal with ordering food. At least I would not starve.

We enjoyed two shows on the main stages. Then we went to a side pavilion near a Jack Daniel's tent. From there we watched a local band from Budapest. It was more comfortable there because the crowd was lighter. I felt a bit more secure.

**10th August, 2007
1:30 p.m.**

This morning I woke up and packed all my gear into my backpack. I went with Eszter to the bus station in town. We are taking a two-hour ride to her hometown of Gyongos where we will meet up with her Dad and her friend Juhger. Her friend Jugher grew up with her, and he started his own line of clothing by the same name. His signature item is a hooded sweatshirt. The hood has bear ears on it. I am saving all my souvenir money. I will go to his shop and spend it on clothes he designed. Then I will bring those back as gifts. Eszter has also scheduled a tennis match between Juhger and I.

10th August, 2007
11:45 p.m.

We arrived in Gyongos. Eszter's dad picked us up at the bus station. Her father and I will have an obvious language barrier as my Hungarian is limited. The only English word I have found him to know is Jack Daniel's. He drove us to his house, and Eszter's car was there waiting. We unloaded our gear into her car.

Eszter and I drove to the park almost as soon as we arrived at her father's home. We met Juhger on a nice set of clay courts. Soccer practice is taking place on the field below. It sounds more like military training as the coach screams in Hungarian. His voice is constant and piercing. He yells at the ten year olds as Juhger and I play our match. I came out on top. Only one person has beaten me at tennis since high school. That is the person who taught me to play, my Dad.

After the tennis match, we go to an apartment building on the other side of Gyongos. Eszter's Dad owns a flat there, and this is where we will stay for the night. We unload our backpacks at the flat. Then we head back over to her father's house. When we pull in the driveway there is a large table out in the driveway and four grills all putting the most delicious smelling smoke into the temperate Hungarian air. They were having a barbeque to welcome me to town. We sat down and began eating chicken, ribs, steaks, and fresh grilled vegetables. It was amazing.

Her dad nudges my shoulder. He then gives me a hand signal to walk with him to a hidden stone cellar. We walk down steps. I duck to miss my head on a stone ledger above the doorway. This cavern is underneath their house. The ceiling, walls, and floor are all made of rock. There are three dusty wooden barrels in the corner. I then notice two of Eszter's father's friends have come down the stairs behind me. I began to feel like Montresor, in Edgar Allen Poe's, The Cask of Amontillado. I tense up.

Her dad grabs a glass off a wooden wall hanger and pumps three shots worth of liquid into the glass. With one sniff I knew that this was Hungarian moonshine. He then hands it to me. Being from Tennessee, I am no stranger to moonshine. I stared at the at the rock ceiling and imagined these Hungarian men had brought me downstairs to the stone vaults to have a good laugh when I coughed it up and shot it out my nose.

With my glass in hand, I pursed my lips and conjured up a mouth full of liquor cutting saliva. This would rest on my tongue to catch the turpentine tasting liquid. I was about to pour it in. I leaned my head back and emptied the entire glass straight down my throat, swallowing quickly. My throat burned like I had just swallowed diesel fuel. I played it off.

I quickly smiled, and said "Yummm!" I acted like it was delicious.

I speak minimal Hungarian. They spoke no English. This group of grown men in the stone cellar was impressed.

11th August, 2007
11:13 p.m.

This was my last day in Hungary. We woke up early and went with Juhger by car for a day in the mountains. Once there we threw Frisbee and visited the highest point in Hungary were I had my picture taken. Then we relaxed at a park.

After the park we went home. I asked Juhger if he would sell me some of his personally designed clothes. From the ATM, I took out the equivalent of about $450. This was roughly 100,000 Hungarian forinth. This was a lot of money. I told him what my plan was, and I laid the 100,000 forinth out on the table. I told him that I wanted to buy 100,000 worth of his Juhger label clothing. Then I would take them back to the United States as gifts. I was going to do this as opposed to buying cheap made tourist trap junk. I ended up with four bear ear hoodies, three hats, four dress shirts, two women's shirts, three fanny packs, and one pair of shorts.

Now Eszter and I are spending the last night at her flat. Her father will take me to the Budapest airport in the morning. On the way to the airport we are going to stop in Budapest and tell Gina and Nora goodbye as well.

12th August, 2007
9:00 a.m.

I am at the airport now and ready to board my flight to New York. I spent the last of my Hungarian money on a sandwich and a book to read on the way home. It is sad to say goodbye.

We all know that there is a real possibility that we may never see each other again, each time we part. They treat me so well and with such hospitality. I am certain that Hungary is one of the best places in Europe to visit. The people are respectful to tourists, everything is reasonably priced, the architecture is first class, and the scenery is gorgeous.

12th May, 2008
3:00 p.m.

Last fall after arriving home from Budapest, I put the rest of my money together and purchased a house. I slowly saved up my money so that I could make a large down payment. It is a small craftsman style house in a lake development in Dandridge. My home features two bedrooms, a bath, and lots of porches.

With my remaining funds I am now planning a trip for the fall of next year. I will go for two weeks and stay in the Netherlands starting at the end of October. I plan to go on this trip solo.

13th September, 2008
11:00 p.m.

   I have great news. My friend Derreck, who lives in Dandridge, has decided to join me on my trip to the Netherlands. He will be with me for the first eight days of my fourteen-day adventure. He booked his plane ticket at my house last night. I will start nailing down our accommodations and activities.

31st October, 2008
1:30 p.m.

   Today Derreck and I fly to Amsterdam. For the entire week we are there I have rented an apartment from a Spanish gentleman. He is about our age. He had a short-term rental apartment listed on Craigslist.
   When I contacted him he told me to send him a down payment. I let him know that this would not be wise of me. Then I asked him what he was going to do while we stayed in his apartment. He told me he wanted to visit his family in Spain. My solution was to have him send me a copy of his passport. Then he told me which flight that he wanted to take to Spain.
   I then booked his plane ticket to Spain on my credit card as a down payment for his apartment. Next, I forwarded him a copy of the ticket. I could now cancel his plane ticket if I arrived in Amsterdam to find the apartment was a hoax. Now the only question is, do we have a place to stay when we arrive in Amsterdam tomorrow morning at 6:45?

1st November 2008
12:30 p.m.

    We arrived in Amsterdam airport this morning on time and in good spirits. Derreck got upgraded to first class and is still tipsy from the free wine. My coach seat was small and cramped as usual. We grabbed our bags. Then we headed for the train so that we could ride into Amsterdam Central station.

    We got off the train and began walking and looking for Herengracht. It was now 8:45 a.m. We had been walking for about 90 minutes. Each of us carried our full luggage. I felt like my arches had flattened out, and I was starting to get sore. Last night was Halloween here. There were witches and goblins passed out all along the canals from the night before. In addition, there was a heap of garbage on the streets and the city crews were working to clean things up.

    After walking in circles for two hours, we finally spotted Herengracht. We deciphered which side of the road 90 Herengracht was on and began counting down street numbers. The name that was on the apartment doorbell was Fernando Navarro. We rang the door and he came down and introduced himself. We walked through the front of a bar, and he took us up the back stairs to his flat.

    It was one room with a bath and full kitchen. There was a full bed and a spare mattress. It was just as he had described, and was perfect for our week in Amsterdam. He let us know we could use anything in his apartment. He then pointed to a closet of his personal possessions that we were not allowed to touch. We said goodbye, and he left for the airport. Derreck and I just woke up from a nap. We are going to grab groceries and walk around.

3rd November, 2008
11:15 p.m.

Today Derreck and I hopped back on the train and made our way to the southern portion of the Netherlands. First, we went to Maastricht and walked around. After walking I decided to take him to a U.S. military cemetery. It was called Maargraten. Over 8,000 American soldiers were buried there during World War Two. We caught a bus to the cemetery. Our destination was about 20 minutes away from the train station.

I noticed the bus stop about the time the bus passed by going full speed. We stood up and took the next stop. We were already two miles away. The walk back to the cemetery took us at least thirty minutes. The foot pains from our opening morning walk around Amsterdam began to return.

By the time we arrived at the cemetery they were closing for the day. I begged the desk clerk to let us take a quick look, because we had traveled a long way. He ultimately relented. We walked through massive concrete pillars. All I could see was a sea of white crosses across the lush green hillside. After taking a moment of silence, we turned around and walked toward the bus stop closest to the entrance of the cemetery. Neither Derreck, nor I, spoke a word.

We caught a nearly empty bus back to Maastricht and boarded the train for

Amsterdam. On our return trip, I nudged Derreck on the train's third stop. We got off the train in Sittard. This was the town where I had studied abroad in 2004. I took a familiar walk down to the city center and told Derreck all about each of the buildings. We ended up at De' Buren. I made a special point not to sit on the register near the bathroom and we ordered drinks and talked.

It was very evocative being back in Sittard after many years away. I somehow felt that any moment one of my classmates might walk through the door. I knew everyone I studied with had long since moved back to his or her homeland. Each person was now deeply immersed in their chosen profession. We sipped the last drops of our beer and boarded the night train back to Amsterdam.

4th November, 2008
11:45 p.m.

Today is the presidential election in the United States. I am twenty-five years old and have been able to vote in two elections. Both of them I have watched the results from the Netherlands. This election both Derreck and I cast early votes so there was no need to send an absentee ballot like I did back in 2004. We are camped out now in our apartment watching CNN. We have an eight pack of Bavaria beer, and we are watching the results.

To make things interesting we made a sidecar bet for drinks. If McCain wins, I will buy his drinks tomorrow. If Obama wins, he has to buy my drinks tomorrow. My bet should not necessarily divulge who my actual ballot was cast for. Just judging by the debates from this fall, I felt like Obama had the advantage. He came off as much more sharp and prepared in the televised debates. Maybe it was just the Teleprompters.

5th November, 2008
11:00 p.m.

Obama won the election. Last night we laid low around our apartment and caught up on much needed sleep. Today, we woke up early and rented bicycles for the rest of our time here. Now we have mobility, and it should help our feet heal. We rode around all day just getting our bearings and learning the town. Tomorrow morning we have tickets to the Heineken museum. I have visited the brewery once before. The last time I was with Brett and Ben. This time the museum and brewery has been closed for two years. During this time, they undertook renovations and remodeling. Tomorrow is the first day that it will re-open. We have tickets to be two of the first fifteen people inside.

6th November, 2008
2:30 a.m.

This morning we rode by bicycle to the Heineken museum. We were the third and fourth people to embark on the new tour. It is only noteworthy because of our rank. It was the first day open. The employees knew just as much as we did. The tour was new to the employees too. We spent most of the tour having to figure out the exhibits ourselves.

After the tour we went to an Irish pub across the street. Derreck had bangers and mash. I enjoyed a shepard's pie. From there we went to Vondel Park, and ended the daylight hours with exploring of the city. We rode our bikes home through rush hour traffic.

Tonight we decided that we wanted to watch local music. I looked up a music venue in our guidebook. While searching for a venue I noticed a list of the top ten bars in Amsterdam. I ran down the stairs and looked out the door. Derreck was still upstairs wondering what I was up to.

I came back up to him pointed out a bar. T'Arendsnest. In the book this bar was located at 90 Herengracht. It was listed as number four on the list of top bars in Amsterdam. Not only did we have a key to front entrance, but we also had an apartment directly up the back staircase for a full week. We made our way down the stairs to the bar. We ordered a beer sampler platter from the bartender. Then we had a prost to our good fortune so far on the trip.

After the visit to T'Arendsnest we moved to another local bar that was one of the top places for live music. I really wanted to catch a good band from around Amsterdam. We went to the bar and paid our cover to get in. We had a few Jack and Cokes and waited for the show to start. They introduced the band. The announcer said that her name was Stacy Epps, and she was from Atlanta, Georgia. We had now traveled thousands of miles to hear music from Atlanta, Georgia.

7th November, 2008
4:00 p.m.

My friend Derreck is a lawyer. He has a zest for international law. I decided taking him to Den Haag would be a good trip. It had been over four years since I went there the first time. We caught a train in Amsterdam around noon and arrive in The Hague there shortly after.

In November, it was really not beach weather. We decided to walk up to the spaceship pier and casino. I pointed out to the exact slot machine where Ben won and lost, in a matter of seconds. We then sat at a Café perched out in the ocean, and enjoyed beverages. Out the windows of the pier we watched the ocean rumble and the clouds frolic. It was a gray November day.

8th November, 2008
10:45 p.m.

Today we rode around Amsterdam on our bicycles and explored. We took in several museums and used the Internet at a café' for around two hours. This is Derrecks last full day. He began to pack up his things. For the evening, we took a final bike ride to an English pub near the central station.

While we were walking around someone pulled Derreck into their bar with an offer of free drinks. I knew better, but I joined him. It was reminiscent of the time in Paris when Max, Bryan, and I were pulled into the McStrip club. However, this was just a bar. We got our free drinks, followed by a tab. The doorman explained that beer was free. A Jack and Coke was twelve Euros each.

When traveling overseas one should always keep in mind that nothing is free, do not accept anything from anyone. They will expect money in return. There are thousands of businesses that earn their living strictly off of unscrupulous practices geared at getting into the wallets of non-native speaking tourists.

We finished up our drinks and then had a beer at an Irish Pub. Derreck and I took our final midnight bike ride alongside the streetlight lit canals of Amsterdam. Then we went back to our apartment on Herengracht.

9th November, 2008
3:00 p.m.

I went with Derreck today to the train station. He set off for the airport. I still have one week left. This is my final night at the apartment. The Spanish man from whom I rented the apartment will arrive back tonight. I will pass him off the key and head to Maastricht by train. I have all my gear packed, and I am ready to go.

Today I cleaned the apartment and everything is spotless. I wanted to make sure that we left everything better than when we came.

10th November, 2008
6:00 p.m.

Last night, around 7:00, I heard a knock at the apartment door. I opened it and it was the gentleman who had rented me the room. I greeted him, told him thanks, and walked my way to the train station. These are the times when traveling only with one backpack works out very well.

I am currently in Maastricht. I caught a train here last night and checked in a hotel. I spent today just walking around town and socializing with whoever would talk to me in either Dutch or English.

11th November, 2008
10:30 p.m.

Today I went to the carnival in downtown Maastricht. The last time I went was with Nora, Gina, Eszter, and Bryan. This year I found a group of Couchsurfers from all over the world that were meeting to go to the carnival together. A gentleman named Frank Verhautz was the organizer, and I joined up with the group. We listened to music and hung out in the Maastricht town center for over eight hours.

I met two interesting girls from New York who were studying in Maastricht. They invited me back to their place for dinner. I just finished hanging out with them. Now I am back at my hotel. Tomorrow I will check out. I am not sure what is next.

12th November, 2008
11:15 p.m.

    I woke up early this morning and ate a typical European hotel breakfast. It consisted of a boiled egg, coffee, and toast. Then I went back up to my room, showered, and packed up my gear. I walked to the train station while reading through my guidebook. I decided to go to Sittard, and then to Arnhem.

    I got off the train in Sittard once more. I rented a bicycle at the same shop I had bought my trusty road bike from years ago. I rode through Sittard and on familiar paths to Watersley hill. I was still able to ride the entire hill without taking a break. Upon reaching the top, I stopped and stared at Watersley, as I caught my breath. I began to realize this was the place I had learned so much about myself just four short years ago.

    None of the buildings, roads, or scenery had changed. It was almost eerie in that my mind was ready at any moment for Bryan, Paul, Ben, Mallory, Eeva, or Liisa to come down the stairs at Watersley, yelling at me to get ready to embark on an adventure. I walked around the halls of Watersley and visited my hallway and kitchen. Then I went down to the bike garage and my Raliegh road bike was still chained to the bike rack, with a flat tire.

    Lost in nostalgia I hopped back on my rented bike, checked my brakes, and whizzed down Watersley hill. I instinctively cycled to Gueweg, and in my head I knew I could walk in the door of the familiar flat and Eszter, Gina, and Nora would be there. I envisioned myself sitting and talking with Brett and Max in their living room.

This was all daydreaming as I rode along the familiar streets of Sittard that I had traversed daily as a 21-year-old college senior. Everyone was now grown up, out of school, and part of their own place in the world. My final stop was at the University. I pulled in and locked my bike to the cold steel rack. The one constant that still remained in Sittard was the delicious university soup and bread.

I turned in my rental bike and boarded the train to Arnhem. I arrived there around 5:30 p.m. I did not know which bus to take to the hostel. I had a map of where it was. I decided to walk. After five miles of walking, I found it. I also took notice of the nearby bus stops so that I would never have to do that again. I checked in my room and had dinner in the lobby restaurant. I am now relaxing in my room and catching up on writing and reviewing my plans for tomorrow.

13th November, 2008
10:30 p.m.

I woke up around 9:00 a.m. this morning and went to the Hoge Veluwe National Park by bus. I paid a small entry fee and there are over 1700 free white bicycles all throughout the park. I rode one for free once I was inside. The park has a circular bike path of 26.7 miles. I took one of the free bikes that the park has available to patrons and embarked on my journey. There are three different cities that have access points to the park along the trail. I rode it straight through and enjoyed the wildlife that included birds, deer, bats, rodents, and bugs.

Once complete I caught a bus back into Arnhem. Along the way I hopped off at a place called the 40-45 Museum. I noticed it on the way to the park. It had a large military tank sitting out front. Once inside, I realized it was a collection of military artifacts from 1940-1945 when Holland was occupied by Germany. The owner did not speak English. A majority of the artifacts were from Germany's forces. It was interesting to see the printed materials from the German propaganda campaign. They looked remarkably the same as the ones that had been used in the United States during the same period.

Some very major battles had been fought in Arnhem. There was even an entire movie about Arnhem and the surrounding area called "A Bridge Too Far" that was based on the battles for the bridges connecting Germany and Holland. This was an interesting museum. I had the place entirely to myself. I thoroughly enjoyed my day today.

14th November, 2008
9:30 p.m.

Today was my last full day in Holland. I am still in Arnhem and this morning I woke up and walked to another museum called the Openlucht Museum. It would translate to Open Air Museum in English. As the Netherlands developed over the last several hundred years many roads, train tracks, and infrastructure were built. As this happened homes and structures came in the way of progress. What this museum would do is acquire the houses and ship them to this property. The museum staff would then erect the homes and make the structure part of the museum. This museum was actually a three-mile wide park with different villages set up of houses ranging from modern to very ancient.

I work in the homebuilding industry, and all the different types of architecture were very interesting. I even found a few log and timber frame homes. The most interesting house here was the Tuberculosis house. It was a very small green box with a window, on a swivel. The idea was that if a relative got sick with Tuberculosis they would be placed in this tiny house. The swivel was so that a family member could turn the house for sunlight to reach the sick family member. The sun's light was supposed to help cure the sickness. The house was placed in the yard. The infected person was isolated from the rest of the family and civilization.

I spent nearly all day here before heading into town to grab my last dinner of the trip. I settled on pizza at a place that my guidebook said was frequented by local students because of affordable prices and fantastic food. It was delicious.

15th November, 2008
10:30 a.m.

I just arrived at Amsterdam's Schipol airport. The train from Arnhem to Amsterdam was so crowed I had to stand for the entire hour and a half ride. I am not sure why, but it might have been the most cramped train ride I have ever taken. I just went through security and I am about to board my flight. Another successful European journey, in the books, literally.

22nd December, 2008
5:32 p.m.

    Last night I went to a Christmas party in Dandridge. It was the Dandridge Men's Cotillion, and it was held at an office downtown. During the party I was munching on food from a cover dish food table. Underneath the tablecloth there was a black Labrador retriever puppy. She had a Christmas ribbon and bow tied around her neck. I estimated she was about four months old, and I kneeled down and petted her. She lifted her head slightly. Then she laid it back down and went to sleep.
    I told the person in line behind me that that she was a really well behaved dog. She was just lying there with over 20 plates of delicious food right above her head. He then informed me that the dog was a stray. They hoped someone from the party would take her home. I told him that if no one had taken her by the end of the night. I would.
    I woke up this morning with a splitting headache. I had a good time at the party. I proceed to shower, eat breakfast, and get prepared for work. After turning off the lights, I was ready to hit the road. I opened my front door, and there was a puppy sized black lab wagging its tail and licking my leg.

Apparently, I brought home a dog last night. I did not have any dog food. I went to my fridge and grabbed lunchmeat. Then I placed it on a tin plate alongside a cereal bowl full of water. This should hold her over while I was at work. My feeling was that if she wanted to stay, she would be there when I got home from work. She was.

**21st June, 2009
2:12 p.m.**

I just planned my next trip to Europe. I am heading to Amsterdam on October 31st. I will be flying back on November 14th. I have plans to go to Spain and Italy on a few side trips. The major cities of this year's adventure will be Amsterdam, Eindhoven, Madrid, Tilburg, and Pescara

**30th October, 2009
5:15 p.m.**

I am taking my last opportunity to throw Frisbee with my black lab Skiddles. This was a given since I would be in Europe for the next fifteen days. I tossed the Frisbee on the opposite side of the field. The neighborhood children who had gathered and were enjoying a temperate, sunny late fall evening. They were playing football and had formed two squads.
Skid sped back with her Frisbee in her mouth panting wildly. She was tired, but nonetheless ready for another toss. During the day she was on the porch. When I got

home from work she was always ready to run. I grabbed the disc once more and gave it a mighty swing. Damn! A wobbler. It landed twenty-five yards from me instead of the typical fifty plus.

From the corner of my eye, I caught some of the football game on the field beside me. The older player tossed a zinger. The football spiraled past all the defender to his lone open receiver in the makeshift, twenty ounce bottle marked, goal line. The receiver crossed his arms like a three-year-old playing catch for the first time. He took the football right to the stomach. He fell to the ground. His teammates were animatedly mad. The defenders gave each other a high five and laughed at him. A sure touchdown had turned into a game altering injury.

Skid brought the Frisbee back and looked at me with a slight dog smile. I had to laugh at the poor kid too. It is not human nature to enjoy someone's pain. We have been trained to enjoy it through such shows as America's Funniest Home Videos and Jackass. In a moment of actual injury, our brain may not be able to decipher between a high definition televison and an actual accident. Either way, if Skid could smile, I could too.

I zinged the next toss much like the way the kid had thrown the touchdown pass. Skiddles cornered the Frisbee in the air and came down with the disc in one graceful motion. The kids took notice while standing around their injured companion. I think I heard a few golf claps. Even the kid crying on the ground took notice.

Skiddles, tired of playing Frisbee toss, zipped past me and ran all the way home and onto our porch. Even she knew it was good to end up on a good note. One thing was clear by her happy demeanor. She had no idea this would be our last exercise together for the next fifteen days. She also possessed zero understanding of her impending visit to the dog sitters tomorrow morning.

The dog followed me into the house. I finalized my packing. This would be my fourth trip to Europe. A half backpack of clothes and gear would be the perfect weight for sightseeing and endless lost walks. One thing I had not packed yet was a newly purchased folding bicycle. The "fiets" as the Dutch called it, is essential to life in the Netherlands. I had rented a bike on my trip last year. This year I would bring a folding bicycle. It was thirty pounds and no larger than a suitcase. This bike would be the ideal foot saver.

I took a quick test ride around the neighborhood. The idea of dismantling this bike and fitting it back into its carry box was daunting. It was much like a tent that had been unpacked and set up. I doubted it would ever fit back into the bag. I decided to work on it later.

Earlier today I had spoken to my mother and father. They wanted to visit with me before I left. I never knew what might happen. Mom arrived home around 6:30 p.m. and Dad would be done with work closer to 7:30 p.m. It was requested that I bring Chinese food for dinner. I brought Subway instead.

I arrived at home and our ever-aging dogs Poco & Jamocha greeted me at my truck door. I like to think that they were thrilled to see me. I could tell by the look in their eye that the plastic Subway bag had exposed my cargo. Their keen sense of smell was working in overdrive. I gave them a Heisman style stiff-arm and made my way to the door. My parents live in a Victorian yellow house that was my home for as long as I could remember.

One year we took a family vacation. My older sister stayed home. She put on the most epic Fourth of July fireworks show Dandridge had ever seen. From this time on, Poco had never been the same. She was now prone to covet shelter of the house at any hint of thunder, fireworks, lawnmower backfire, BB gun, or a minor lightning strike up to fifty miles away. I provide this information, because my parent's home was now a fortress. The exterior was primarily designed to keep Poco out. The wrap around porch had gates akin to wooden prison bars. All the outside doors were reinforced with a bulletproof style Plexiglas. To say that my father had rebuilt every door on the house at least a dozen times was not a lie. To say that loco Poco would never chew, claw, and ram them down again, was a lie too.

I waltzed in through the mudroom of their home. It was still clean from the shining it took before my younger sister wedded Tyler Robinson two weeks earlier. I made my way to the kitchen and Mom was ready for a hug. I obliged. We chatted and competed in a tense Jeopardy match. While we ate our food we skipped the buzzers and just blurted out the answers. Sometimes when we knew them, and even when we just thought we did.

The second category popped up and it was, European Union. It was a shame that this was not my day to actually be on the show. I drilled the category until last question popped up.

"Daily Double!" Said Alex.

I wagered everything I had previously won, which was nothing.

Alex spoke again. "The city in western Europe where the European Union treaty was ratified,"

"What is Maastricht!" I exclaimed.

I studied twenty miles north of there during my educational vacation of my senior year. I had been there over twenty times to watch NFL football and visited there twice last year. I also had plans to be there again in eleven days.

Bzzzt! "What is Denmark?" the fat lady, Tina guessed.

It was wrong and Alex called upon another gentleman, "What is Luxemburg?" said the man, and this was incorrect too.

The question timed out and Trebek explained that Maastricht was the correct response.

The kitchen table erupted with high fives and Mom shook up her twenty ounce Diet Dr. Pepper and sprayed it on my head like I had just won the Indy 500. Ok, not really.

She did say, "We need to get you on this show."

This is a reciprocal compliment we use when either one of us truly smoke a category. After this I quickly cooled off on correct answers and engaged in small talk with Mom.

During this talk she told me how excited she was about my trip. Then she made me promise that the next time I travel to Europe that I would take her with me. I agreed to this. At the same instant, Dad called. He would be home in about thirty minutes. We finished our food and moved our gathering to the den.

My father arrived a short time after. I gave him a hug and a copy of my itinerary and passport. I also promised to e-mail whenever possible.

31st October, 2009
2:00 p.m.

My alarm clock rang. It was now the first day of my trip. I grab my bags and throw them in my truck. Skid jumped in the truck like it was her normal everyday routine and perched in the passenger seat. I locked the door to my home and closed the front gate. I tossed a bag of dog food and a leash into the bed of my truck.

My country, lake view home is on the edge of a peninsula jutting into Douglas Lake. The farmland I must travel has more than enough smells to keep an over active black lab completely immersed for the entire drive. As we ride to the dog sitter's house, Skid is enjoying a cold whiff of deer, Shetland pony, dog, horse, goat, goose, and cow scented air. She has her head hung out the window like dogs will do.

I hop out of the truck at the dog sitter's home and put the leash and dog food on the porch. I opened the passenger door and lead

Skid to the gate. She now comes to grips with the depth of my plot. The horror she experiences when she finally realizes she is being left behind gives me chills. Skiddles is certain she has been abandoned again, and I will not be coming back. Her cries and whimpers permeated through the wooden latch gate.

I launch a customary, "My dog is at your place," text message.

I completed my work for the day around 11:00 a.m., and I shot the gap. This is what we call it at the office when someone shows up for work on time, but leaves earlier than they are supposed to by heading out the moment any opportunity is presented. From work I drove to the Dandridge free parking lot. I met my friend Josh Greene and his girlfriend, Leah. He is twenty minutes late, as usual, but is nice enough to take me to the airport. I let it slide, and slip him a 20 dollar bill for his generosity.

We arrived at the airport. Josh snapped a photo of me as I walked away.

Leah and Josh started screaming, "I love you Jobe!" loud and repetitively.

Everyone at Knoxville's Mcghee Tyson Airport turned around to check on the commotion. Red faced, I passed the airport clerk my passport. A TSA agent was sipping coffee behind me. I placed my fold up bike bag into the screening queue. Honestly, I am not sure it will hold up through the bag handlers tossing, cramming, stuffing, and punting it across the ocean.

My flight is about to board and the TSA has just announced that they will be screening passengers once more as they proceed to the gate. I walk up and handed them my passport and boarding pass once again. One of the TSA agents asked me if Washington DC was my final destination. Usually people in this type of position know the answer to any question before they ask. I told her I was going to Amsterdam.

    She said, "Have a nice trip."

31st October, 2009
3:30 p.m.

    Landing in Washington D.C. I thought about my colleague in the log home industry, Grace. She lives in Washington D.C.

    I send out a Party In The USA text to "I hop off the plane at IAD, with a dream and a cardigan."

    I proceed to my gate and get seated. Then I take one last look at my phone.

    I received a response from her. "Welcome to the land of politics, are you going to fit in?"

    I cannot remember the next line of this Miley Cyrus song to save my life, which is probably a good thing. I cannot reply back. Then my phone rings. It was Grace. She tells me of her recent promotion and Redskins football news. I inform her about my trip, and the announcement comes for me to board the plane.

    I boarded, but not before I bounced out the final text of my time in the United States. "I jump off the tram at Gate C, for the third time. Look to the right and I see a Five Guys sign."

    I turn off my phone and fly out of my cell phone's service area for the next fifteen days.

31st October, 2009
5:00 p.m.

My flight began as I sat down in my seat without anyone beside me. I thought how nice it would be to have extra legroom. Just as the last people boarded the plane a guy about my age placed his luggage in the overhead. He occupied the seat adjacent to me. I wondered if he was a Dutchman or American.

The only advantage of long international flight is that it gives me a good opportunity to brush up my Dutch during the flight. After not having heard the language for almost a year. I found out the guy next to me is Mark. He studied in Seattle and grew up in DC. He was traveling with his Dad and brother for a male bonding trip to Amsterdam. Good enough, I had someone next to me to talk to during the flight.

31st October, 2009
12:15 p.m.

I watched movies, ate food, and listened to a crying baby choir duel it out over the next eight hours. I arrived at Schipol airport in Amsterdam. It was 7:00 a.m. in the morning. My main worry is what I was going to do for the first five hours while I waited for my room to come available in Amsterdam. I got off the plane and walked through the terminal. From there I went through customs. The agent at the desk reviewed my passport with twenty plus country stamps and stared me in the eye.

He said, "Is this really you?"

I removed my hat and acknowledged it was me. He stamped my passport as I proceeded through the airport. I was waiting at the rollers for my bike bag. I had severe doubts that my bike would arrive here in one piece. Luggage after luggage came out of the shoot. Some bags were busted open other were taped shut. Others in plastic cling wrap, which was an ominous sign. Finally, I noticed the Rock and Roll Bicycle logo as it rolled slowly around the perimeter to my location. I snatched it from the rollers and proceeded to use the in airport ATM.

I took out 260 euros and this was the equivalent of about 400 US dollars at the time. My total budget for the two weeks was 1,900 US Dollars. When I count my remaining money while traveling I only recognized what is still in the bank. Cash in my pocket goes really quickly. For me to count it as still available seemed irresponsible. I should say that I have 1500 dollars for 15 days, and a wad of euros in my pocket to get me started.

My first purchase was a train ticket to Amsterdam's Central train station. I boarded the train and found a seat. The bike and bag were heavier than I anticipated. I arrived at my stop and walked out on to the street and tried to locate a good location to assemble my steel horse. It had rained recently. I was forced to choose the driest, wettest location. I was going to have to sit and kneel to get the bike assembly completed. The bike went together effortlessly. I was down to the last pedal. I tried to screw in the pedal for at least 15 minutes. Then I came to the conclusion that it must be stripped.

Just as I stood up, I was asked for directions. My bike building location turned out to be right underneath the city map at Amsterdam central station. The girl who asked was from California. I am now playing tour guide. My study abroad, and the additional week here in Amsterdam last year has me to the point were it is easy to tell her where she needs to be. First the California girls, and then a group of girls from Georgia needed help. I am now back to working on my bike.

I dig out my tool kit and turn the pedal with my vice grips. It was still not accepting the pedal. I decide to trek three hundred yards to a bike rental store. This was the same store that Derreck and I rented from last year. A young man is standing outside and looks at the pedal in my hand and I tell him it is stripped.

He says, "Do you want a new pedal?"

I shook my head, "yes."

He tells me that, "Today is your lucky day, because everything is free before we open."

He hands me a new pedal, and I thank him. I walk back to my bike juggling the two left pedals. I think about how generous he was. I go back to the bike and begin my attempt to install my gift. I turn it, and nothing happens just like the last pedal. My mind assembles the equation of the two new pedals not working. I try to turn it the opposite way. It goes into place. There was nothing wrong with either pedal. The installer was trying to screw it in backwards. I decided to keep my spare pedal on hand as I took my first morning ride through the city of Amsterdam.

I decided to stay at Bob's Hotel since I was traveling alone. It would be essential to meet people if Halloween was going to be fun. My room is very close to the station, and very low cost. I go into the lobby and check in. I made make my second purchase of the trip, a bed. I cannot use it until noon. I go in search of a light breakfast and stop in a juice bar. A twelve-ounce glass of orange juice pressed from at least twenty orange halves does the trick. I go back to relax in the lobby of the hotel. There are plenty of tables, and the ever-popular free breakfast is going on.

It was now 10:00 a.m. as I walked in the lobby door. Every table is jam-packed. There is one table with open seats. I ask if I can sit.

The guy says, "Do you want food?"

He thinks I am homeless and just trying to scrounge a free breakfast. I declined breakfast and ask him where he is from.

He says, "California."

So that is what I will call him since I do not recall his name. We begin to chat about Amsterdam, my study abroad, and his recent move to Antwerp, Belgium to live with his family.

Two more guys sit down in the previously open seats to my left and right. They begin eating toast and hard-boiled eggs. They are from Louisiana and Wisconsin, and this is what they will be referred to. Wisconsin and Louisiana are studying French in Paris and already both look more pretentious and perhaps fully immersed in the French culture.

I cannot make fun of them, because I was mistaken as a homeless guy just five minutes before.

We continue to chat as another guy pulls up a chair. He placed a full tub of butter, a glass of chocolate milk, and a stack of eight pieces of white bread on the table. He sat down and began to butter the bread. At this time, California excused himself to walk up the street to an Internet café. I asked the newest member of our makeshift ensemble what his name is.

He butters his bread and says "Louis, and I am from Montreal Canada."

This was muttered with bread butter and chocolate milk filling his mouth. Louisiana, Wisconsin, and I engage Louis in conversation. I sit back and relish in the fact that I finally made it on my vacation. I work fifty weeks a year and get two off, what a deal.

Louis butters another piece of bread and tells us about the city where he lives, Amsterdam. A worker at Bob's asks him something. I begin to think he works here. Louis takes another heaping load of the butter and begins the final shaping in preparation for a dip in his chocolate milk. He dips it, then he stuffs it in his mouth. Immediately he began telling a story.

It seems that one time he was at Hamilton Beach, California when he was eleven. He caught a wave. The lead singer from the Red Hot Chili Peppers came up and punched him in the mouth. All the while, spitball sized chunks of butter, chocolate milk, and bread are spraying across the table like laser beams.

Louis who is now standing up with his hands in the air is proclaiming, "I was only eleven! The fucker punched me in the face!"

This scene was actually from the movie Point Break. No one called him out on it. Nonetheless, it was a novel tale and the fact that Louis had just taken a scene from a well-known movie and adopted it as his own will always be a memory for me. This was hilarious and worrisome at the same time.

It is now noon. Louis is down to two pieces of bread, and a half tub of butter. The chocolate milk seemed to never lose a drop. Even after five pieces of butter bread dunking it is still full. I was about to get up when Louis began.

Louis started his story like this. "The Queen of England went across the Atlantic Ocean and gave Eisenhower a blowjob."

Then he proceeded to explain the entire gamete of American history. He bounced from Christopher Columbus to the Trail of Tears. Then he moved to present day politics in less than two minutes. He seemed educated, but at the same time knew nothing of factual importance.

"American history by Louis!" I exclaimed.

Wisconsin and Louisiana were uncontrollably laughing by this point. Another slice of bread and gobs more butter were laid flat. Louis began a new story about his cat Mimi. It is so weird how people talk about their animals while doing the hoochey oooee gooee animal voice. It was the same voice. It was only produced by a grown man in public, with a mouth full of chocolaty butter bread. By this time, we were strictly using Louis for the entertainment value. We asked loaded questions, and he gave loaded answers.

1st November, 2009
3:30 a.m.

    I checked into my room after breakfast and fell immediately to sleep. When I woke, I instinctively opened my cell phone. It told me that my SIM card was rejected. I had no coverage. The time was 12:16 p.m. back home in Tennessee. I got up and took a shower. Then I walked back down to the lobby. There was Louisiana and Wisconsin sitting at the same table as if they had never left. I sat down and asked them what they were doing tonight for Halloween. They had heard about a pub-crawl during a walking tour they took. This sounded fun, as long as a guide showed up.
    I then told them about a college football game that was on at a Sports Satellite Bar in the Leidsplein area. I asked them to see their map so we could coordinate the pub-crawl and football game into one trip. Great! They were both in the same area so we walked to use the ATM and got tickets for the tram ride there.
    We hopped on the tram and motored over to the Leidsplein area of Amsterdam and got off at our stop. We watched dancers in the square, watched a guy dressed as Pac Man using the ATM, and located both the sports bar and the first bar of the pub crawl. They were directly across from each other so we sat on the patio of the sports café and watched college football. After two beers and a burger,

we proceeded to the pub-crawl. The bar had just opened at 9:00 p.m. The line was forming out the front. A guy dressed up as the Joker from Batman came up carrying a pumpkin. He pulled out a knife. I thought I was about to get mugged. Then he hand carved the pumpkin on the spot. I now admire his ingenuity and skill that was used to create this international Halloween tradition.

We entered the bar and we were fed free drinks of red vodka punch. Then we were each given a token for the drink of our choice at the bar. This time it was a Jager shot. After posting up at the best table in the club we watched the people pile in. All counted two hundred and fifty people had joined the crawl. At twenty Euros per person I could imagine the entrepreneur behind this Halloween pub-crawl menacing his fingers and smiling. He had created a huge group of Halloween revelers. He convinced each of them to pay 20 euros by employing salespeople dressed in Halloween costumes to sell tickets throughout the day in Amsterdam. It was brilliant.

By now the club was overloaded. Dancing, free drinks, costume party shenanigans were the new normal. Three nuns, a bloody sexy nurse, and a fall fairy floated around the mob of fake police, zombies, and Pac-man. Neither me, nor California, or Wisconsin were dressed in costume. Party foul, I know, but I did not think I would have any room for a costume. The only thing I could think of was to borrow a Barrack Obama mask from my friend, Matt Keaton, at home. Not because I was particularly crazy about the man, the President, or the person, but it would have been simple and easy to tote.

It seems like everyone in Europe has given Obama a free pass ever since he was introduced as a candidate. I spent the 2004 and 2008 elections in Holland, and I fully understand both sides of the dynamic. Either way, I never got around to asking for the mask. Here I sit without a costume. Whenever someone asked about my costume, I told them I was a Romanian dressed up like an American. I also came complete with a southern accent.

We proceeded to the next bar, and it was called The Pirate Ship. Yes, real pirates ran the underground bar. The ceiling was that of a typical pirate ship. It was complete with circular windows, a plank, and scallywags-a-plenty. We got a token at this bar and received a beer. Then we took more shots of the red vodka drink. This time however the bottle touched my lip when they poured. It grossed me out. I could only imagine how many others had touched it as well. Nonetheless, I did not let a single slip like that ruin my night. One, it was free. Two, the girl who made the mistake was hot. Three, it was a pub-crawl on Halloween, in Amsterdam.

Now the bartenders have taken the microphone and thank everyone for coming to their bar in a killer pirate voice. They proceed to light two torches. The crowd inside roars and the bar is in hysteria. Woooooof!!!! The flame erupts in to an explosion from both sides of the bar. Is this a repeat of the Great White concert in Rhode Island from 2003?

Oh nevermind, it was just the bartenders spitting fire. Holy shit! They are actually spitting fire, Wooooof!!!... Wooof!!!!.... Wooooof!!! The bar is electric with excitement and roars with enjoyment. Then the DJ lays down a beat and the dancing commences. Louisiana takes off and goes scouting. I knew he had a little bit of bird dog in him, or at least some Cajun coon dog. I am sandwiched between a Martian girl and a cheerleader dancing. Louisiana motions to me. We head outside so we can find the next bar.

Amsterdammed, yes, I will be. This is also the name of the next bar, and we get free beers there too. I start dancing once more. I skip the red community vodka this time around. I am now dancing with smoking hot blond from Boston. I am doing my typical one leg straight, one leg moving gangster shuffle. I hold my hand up in the air to conduct the crowd. One problem, I forgot the conductor hand was also holding my beer. I spilled my entire beer on her head. I tried to apologize to her. I reasoned with her that I got bumped. Game over, I exit the bar.

As I stood outside the bar, I began talking to an Irish girl, and her boyfriend. She just kept telling me how much she loved American boys right in front of him. She did not like the country, or the food, just an American boy. She said this over and over. Her poor boyfriend makes me think of those times when people act like I am invisible. I do admire his girlfriend's honesty.

Next we moved to a bar, that turned our group down. The pub-crawl had grown too large. Fire code would dictate that we moved our party to an alternate location, so we all followed. During our walk we passed the sports bar from earlier. I stopped briefly to check scores.

After rejoining the group, we arrived at the next bar. Here we were served yet another free beer. This time my inhibitions were gone. I was rapidly reaching my limit. I had one more red vodka shot. This was the final bar of the crawl and our friends, the nuns, won the 500-euro prize for the best costume. I now realize the other side of the entrepreneur's pub-crawl scheme. It was the nuns who sold tickets at the first bar. The costume contest was rigged. The winner of the 500-euro prize worked for the actual pub-crawl company.

The night is finished and we must now trek home, and it is 3:00 a.m. The tram stopped at midnight. We walked back to our hotel as a group. I bid farewell to Wisconsin and Louisiana. I wished them the best of luck in their study abroad.

Many friendships are quick and instant when one travels. An interaction, a meal, or a free pedal can all spark a friendship. This friendship may only last a moment. Then it leaves quickly like fleeting sobriety.

1st November, 2009
9:30 p.m.

This morning I awoke in my bed around 9:00 a.m. I packed all my gear and went down to the lobby where I proceeded to skip breakfast. I walked to the Albert Heijn grocery market and picked up a box of strawberry juice and Jong Gouda cheese. I then went back to the hotel and grabbed a hard-boiled egg and bread to go with it. Sorry, no chocolate milk and buttered bread. I did drink straight from my jug of strawberry juice. This also makes me wonder why I cannot find 100% strawberry juice in the United States. It is delicious. I drink it like water, whenever I am in Europe.

    I hop on my bike and rode it to the train station where I pack it neatly into its bag by removing the seat, handlebars, and pedals. I purchased a ticket to Eindhoven, and head to the platform. This bike is again heavier than I remembered. Now it is also fully loaded down with tools, a chain, and a lock. I boarded the train and proceed to Eindhoven where I plan to couchsurf with a local.

    Couchsurfing is a network of people that open their couches to others. They also are able to use other people's couches in the network. I had found a host in Eindhoven, near the airport. This way I could have a place to stay and wake up for my early flight to Madrid tomorrow.

    I disembarked the train and carried my bike bag to the front of the station. I assembled it down to the left pedal, which went in smoothly. I quickly checked on the station map and looked for the street. This was where my Couchsurfing host lived. By doing this I could locate the address. I also might be lucky enough to find an Internet café. My goal was to ride into the Eindhoven city center. Once there I would lock my bike and locate an Internet café. Then I could find out what time I needed to meet my Couchsurfing host, Nichon.

I hopped upon my bike and pedaled up to the street corner. I was in front of the Eindhoven Central Station. My bike lane got the green light on the bicycle traffic signal. I gave the pedals a firm downward stroke. The pedal fell to the pavement and spun like a top for a brief moment.

There is no feeling quite like having a bike break in the middle of a busy street. I gathered the pedal from the intersection and retreated back to the sidewalk. I put the kickstand down and began the familiar left pedal adjustments. I grab my pedal. I had a bit of difficulty threading it. It was completely stripped.

I struggled on the ground. I glanced up to see a guy who looked like Jesus with glasses. He sat on a bike. I continue trying to turn the pedal and looked up again. I hear the eye glassed Jesus engage his kickstand with a common sound of steel, springs, and concrete. He pulls out a metal bar and a three-inch piece of what looked like a garden hose. Without saying a word he grabs the pedal from me. Then he placed the hose material in the stripped groves of the pedal socket and threaded the pedal in. I thank him as he walks away and mounts his bike.

He then says, "You must tighten it now."

I reached down and tightened the pedal with my adjustable crescent wrench. I looked up seconds later, and he was gone.

I was now on the road again and searching for my host's home. Over the next three hours I biked, walked, walked some more, biked some more, biked, walked, and tried fruitlessly to find an Internet café. I asked upwards of two-dozen strangers where I could find an Internet café. They all looked at me like I was an idiot.

  Beaten down and tired I mounted my bike and headed back to the central station. As I was riding I thought about asking the train kiosk staff. They spoke fluent English and may have insight. I entered the station and went up to the available desk. I made my query.

  The lady who sold tickets at the train station told me there was a restaurant upstairs. The eatery had pay by the hour Internet computers. I could have used that information when I arrived three hours ago and skipped the run around. The lengthy tour of the Eindhoven may prove valuable later. Also my pedal might have broken at a time when there was not someone standing ready to assist.

  I went upstairs to the café and ordered a coffee and thirty minutes of the Internet for around three euros. I got on the computer and found that I was to meet the Couchsurfing host at another Café in town. I searched Google Maps for the street and walking path from the station. I studied the details and wrote down the important turns. Then I proceeded to write e-mails to my parents and friends. My time was up. It was now 3:00 p.m. I was supposed to meet my host at 5:00 p.m. at the café.

  Re-mounted on my bike, I began riding into the city once more. I found the street the café was on quickly. I then realized it connected at the street my host lived on. I decided to park my bike where the streets connected and walk to find the café. After locking up my bike I strolled down the street and looked for the café. I found three or four eateries. I started to think about what was the name of the place I am looking for. I pulled out my trusty scrap of paper with details of the rendezvous on it. All I had on the paper was, Klein Street. Apparently, I only wrote down the street name and not the actual name of the café.

I began using deductive reasoning to rule out several cafes. I decided it must be the Grand Café, which I am standing right in front of. I sat at a table on the front of the café, as it began to rain. It is now 4:45 p.m. I watched the passing people to try and match them to the Couchsurfing profile picture. I am unsuccessful and now it is 5:15 p.m. If I cannot find my host, I have no bed. I decide to find her house based on the address that I have. I pulled out my scrap paper of information.

I unlocked my bike and rode in what had turned into pouring rain. I found Monteloos, which was noted on my scrap paper.

It said, "The flat is right behind Monteloos, Number 116."

I looked at the street number and I am at 118...120...122. It was now time for a U-turn. After riding ten feet in the opposite direction my bike is directly in front of Monteloos. I follow a brick wall down a path. I noticed 116 E on the wall. I push down the kickstand and hop off of my bike. The anxiety was overwhelming as I knocked on a strange door in a foreign country. A lady opens the door,

"Nichon?" I said.

This was the name on the info scrap. She said that she was Nichon. Then she invited me in. I walked inside and placed my backpack on the floor. She asked me if I needed a towel to dry off, because the rain had soaked me sufficiently. I told her no, and she offered me a seat at her kitchen table. I took the seat and she asked if I would like something to drink. I requested coffee, and she quickly went to work on the stove with an old fashion coffee percolator.

    I brought her a gift of University of Tennessee gloves, and a CD of music from Tennessee. I decided to give them to her at this time to show goodwill. She smiled, looked at the the strangely colored orange gloves. Then she placed the CD in the CD-Rom of her computer. We began to talk.

    She said she was about to make bread when I arrived. Then she was going to get ready to meet me at the café. I then told her I was at the Grand café and thought she might have suggested it. She said that the café I was supposed to meet her at was actually called The Baron. Then she mentioned that it was not five o'clock yet. This was the moment I realized I had been the victim of another European Daylight Saving Time. I reasoned it was better to be an hour early at the wrong café than an hour late at the correct one.

    Nichon made dinner, and we played a card game. After this we went across the alleyway to her photo studio. I helped her on one of her university projects she was doing called, Taste.

    She said, "People are tested growing up for sight, touch, hearing, and smell, but taste was greatly neglected."

    Her vision was to make a line of food that had a label that included the recommended amount of chews to maximize taste. I found this idea was novel. I took almost one thousand shots of her in the studio eating an apple down to the core with her expensive camera.

We then walked back to her flat and I took a shower before we watched the movie Nixon Vs. Frost. We decided it was time for bed. I had a 9:00 a.m. flight and would need to be up early. She helped me inflate my air mattress. I gave her a hug goodnight, and goodbye. She then got in the shower. I took this time to write a thank you card and decorate a U.S. one dollar bill. I placed them both inside an envelope. Then I stashed it on top of her fruit bowl before I fell asleep.

2nd November, 2009
11:53 p.m.

The alarm clock came early. I hopped on my bike and headed to the central train station to catch a bus to the airport. I got lost and ended up next to the PSV Eindhoven professional soccer stadium. From there I listened and watched until a train went by. I turned my bike in that direction.

I ended up in bike tunnel. When I came back to daylight on the other side there was the main bus station in all its glory, right in front of me. I took my bike and chain and locked it to a rack with at least five hundred other bikes. I took my bike bag and chained it to the bike rack as well. I stashed my tool bag in the pack so that everything was covered. Then I threw my backpack on my shoulder and went inside the bus station.

Once inside the bus station I walked to the bus information desk. I asked which bus went to the airport. It was bus 401 the employee told me with his finger pointing towards the large 401 sign right beside me. The sign had a picture of an airplane and Airport in huge letters. I went into the Albert Heijn grocery store in the station and bought a drink. I waited for the bus, and I sipped my drink. Then it arrived.

As I tried to validate my bus ticket, the driver took off. I found myself falling slightly towards a seat so I took it. This would be a free bus ride. I could see the upcoming stops. One of them was called The Flight Forum. The bus stopped and I hopped off. I got my bearings moments later and realized I had gotten off two stops too soon. I used the next seconds to watch the path of the bus so that I could follow its way on foot.

This is why when traveling in a foreign country it is obligatory to always be early. In Europe it seems that no body is ever on time or in a hurry. In the case of an American traveling abroad and making connections, on time, is usually too late. I had learned this the hard way in the London airport years ago on my way to Paris.

As the sun was shining over the horizon, I walked across a slight hill and located the Eindhoven Airport sign. It was a welcome sight. I walked in and checked into my flight. I went through security and boarded my flight to Madrid.

We touched down in Spain, and I had the name of the hotel I wanted to stay at in my bag, along with a map. My only decision now was to take the bus or the underground. They both met at the same platform so I walked that direction. It was probably a mile total. I was still in the airport. I finally came to the metro entrance. I noticed an information office. I asked the lady if she spoke English.

She gave the common European answer, "A little."

I asked her how to get to my hotel, and showed her my map. She gave me a subway route map and plotted out my journey. Then she even showed me which button to press on the ticket machine. I got my ticket and went through the gate. Then I boarded the metro. After two transitions I made it to my stop. I got off the subway and walked up the stairs to the brightly sun lit streets. It was bustling outside. I needed a map to get my bearings once I emerged from the subway.

I found a map of Madrid. After staring stupidly for five minutes, I realized it was a bus route map. I decided to walk in the direction I thought the hotel would be in. After half of a mile, I found a more detailed map. I looked up the road name in the legend. Then I located the coordinates on the map. I was close. I crossed the street, walked up 300 yards, and spotted the street on my right. I crossed through traffic and began checking the house and street numbers. I located the hotel on my left and went to check in at the desk.

After dropping my gear in my room I decided to stroll into town and get food, take a picture or two, and find a place that had the Internet. The map I had brought from home had an Internet café listed on it so I trekked in that direction. I first found a McDonald's and ordered three barbeque chicken sandwiches in Spanish.

The cashier said, "Are you American?"

He must have caught a slight Mexican accent in my Spanish. Then he traced it back to North America.

I ate my food and continued on my way. I was now walking down Gran Via. I had imagined this was Madrid's main road. I walked for nearly three miles alongside thousands of other locals and tourists. I never found the café mentioned in book. I decided to cross the street and see if maybe it was on the other side. I found a cross walk and began to walk back for nearly a mile when I noticed an orange and white sign that said telifonica, Internet, fax.

The building was no wider than my arm span. The walls were lined with souvenirs and coolers of drinks. I grabbed a Coke and asked for the Internet. She pointed downstairs, and I walked down. It was a cramped area with eight computers and two telephone booths. There was a lady screaming and crying in Spanish. She gave the Internet café employee royal Hell. For what? I will never know.

I ordered thirty minutes of Internet and sent my Dad an e-mail to tell him I was fine. Then I proceeded to look at all the usual sites of my daily surf. I checked Google Finance, Yahoo, the weather, and E-Trade. I had five minutes left when I realized I needed to plan my trip back to the airport while I was here. It was now Monday. By Tuesday at bedtime, I would have to secure my transportation to the airport. My flight back to Eindhoven left at 5:45 a.m. This departure time was before public transportation was in operation. I Googled, Madrid Airport Transportation Options, and found info of a bus terminal that served only the airport. I marked it on my Madrid city map and decided to search for it the next day when I was exploring. My Internet minutes were up. Now the lady who was crying when I walked in had the Internet café attendant in tears. I decided it was time to go.

    I walked back to the hotel. It was now 5:00 p.m. I turned on the TV and eventually dozed off. I woke up about an hour ago and took a shower and walked down to the lobby. From here I proceeded to search for food, and I ended up at the center with the same McDonald's but decided to try something different. Next door was Burger King. I ate a three-euro, Big King Cheeseburger. It was fantastic.

    I then walked back to the hotel and read a book in the lobby till midnight. It sounds kind of boring, but I felt it was my best bet. I would have plenty of nightlife in Tilburg when I returned to the Netherlands. Plus partying by myself could be dangerous, because of my lack of Spanish language skills. I could easily become part of someone's plot to do bad without even knowing. After each drink one loses inhibition. Eventually all warning signs blend in as part of the party. Tomorrow would be my first and last full day in Madrid. It was a short trip, and I needed to be fresh. For thirty euros it was hard to pass up the flight and experience of visiting this robust city. Even if the duration was only two days.

3rd November, 2009
10:30 p.m.

    No alarm clock was needed this morning. I brushed my teeth and proceeded out the door. I had marked a map the night before of where I wanted to take pictures. I covered many miles over the next five hours. I shot over eighty pictures. One picture alone I marched over one mile out of the way to get. I wanted a photo of the water. It was ugly when I got there, but I still snapped the picture.
    I then found a small market. I purchased an apple, a can of strawberry juice, cheese, and fresh baked roll. I paid my four euros and searched for a place to eat. I was thirsty so I cracked open my aluminum can of strawberry juice. This had a strange taste. It turned out the drink was a wine cooler. It was all I had. I just had to make sure I was in a place that I could eat without getting stopped for drinking on the street at 11:12 a.m. I was in the middle of the Place De La Mayor. I sat down at the center of the square and devoured my apple, cheese bread sandwich, and drank my strawberry beer. This was a true vacation and relaxation. I took the moment to take a deep breath. I marked areas I had already walked on my map. Then I plotted my afternoon trek.
    I decided that I still needed to find my airport transportation so I tried to locate the bus station and review their schedule. I walked towards the Plaza De Colon. It was under heavy construction. After an hour of walking, I admitted defeat of not being able to find the bus station. I then took a metro ride

back. After seven hours of walking, I rode the metro for four minutes. I was back at my hotel's metro stop. This ride only cost one euro. It was truly efficient, but it is hard to scout a city while riding in an underground concrete tube. I arrived at my stop and went back to the hotel. I grabbed a bottle of water and took a break in the lobby.

After my break, I decided I would go use the Internet. On the way back from my walk yesterday, I noticed several other Internet cafés. These were much closer. I walked out of the lobby once more down Gran Via. I arrived at the Internet café closest to my hotel and wrote e-mails. I sent one to my father and one to Liisa who was from Finland. I had lived in the same apartment complex at Watersley. She now attended the University of Tilburg in the Netherlands and was working on a graduate degree. I would be Couchsurfing with her for a few days. I got the specifics on where to meet her tomorrow. I then looked up the cost of a taxi to the airport. The general rule was 20 to 30 euros. I had about 30 euros in my pocket, but I decided to re-up at the ATM so I could avoid a sticky situation. I had now determined a cab was going to be the best option. I had to be at my gate an hour early. I would need to wake up at 4:00 a.m.

I went to the ATM and found a newsstand with an English paper. I bought it to read and went back to my hotel. It was 6:00 p.m. I packed and began to read the paper. Half way through the business section, I remembered I had forgotten to eat while I was out. I left the hotel once more and found a Spanish sandwich shop. I had a large specialty sandwich with cheese, chicken, onions, jalapeno, lettuce, honey mustard, and fries. I went back to the hotel, took a shower, and set my alarm for 4:12 a.m. then walked to the lobby to line up my cab and finish my newspaper.

I finished up the paper around 8:00 p.m. and went to the desk and asked them for a cab at 4:15 a.m. They had absolutely no clue what I said.

I wrote down, "Taxi 4:15 a.m." Then I pointed to it on a sheet of paper.

She walked over to pay phone, and I handed her my change. She put the money in and dialed the number. It was the wrong number. I handed her more money. The phone connected and she handed it to me. It was a blur of Spanish. I did not understand what the person on the other end said.

"Parlay Englais" I said.

"No," said the voice on the other end of the phone.

We exchanged several more minutes of similar conversation that was not understood. I had to add more money just to keep going. I flagged the desk clerk back over from behind the front desk.

She came over and I told her, "Aueroporto, 4:15 a.m."

She spoke for a moment to the cab company and gave me a head nod. I went upstairs and went to sleep.

**4th November, 2009.
11:17 p.m.**

I woke up early before the alarm. I was out the door at 4:00 a.m. with a cold Coca-Cola from the lobby drink machine. There was a vacant taxi sitting on Gran Via. I decided to leave my called cabby hanging and get a fifteen-minute jump on the airport.

I knocked on the window of a sleeping Spanish cab driver and demanded, "Aeropeurto, undelay, undelay!"

He nodded, "Yes."

I loaded up my bag. On the way to the airport we listened to the local radio. It was always strange the music mix that plays on European radio. We arrived at the airport and the total came to 35 euros. Any good cab driver can find a way to go the long way around and put the meter on the high end of the estimated price range. That is why I generally avoid them. I stick with bikes, walking, and public transportation while visiting Europe.

I walked into the airport and went through the typical security screening. Then I made my way onto my flight back to Eindhoven. As I sat on the plane, I began to review my next steps once I made it to Eindhoven. After landing I would need to hop on the bus from the airport. I would take the bus to the train station. From there I could unlock my bike.

We arrived at Eindhoven airport. I got off the plane. I boarded the bus and again did not stamp my bus ticket. After arriving at the train station, I would locate my bike. I got off the bus at the station. I walked down the row where I thought I had locked my bike. I walked another row and looked at the nearly endless array of cycles. Still, there was nothing. It began to rain.

I continued to scour the bike racks for the next thirty minutes. Surely, I was at the wrong racks. I then decided to grab food, and clear my mind. I went into the train station and had breakfast. I watched music videos a T.V. in the station while I mentally retraced my steps.

After eating I went back outside to search again. I looked to no avail, still nothing. I decided to retrace my steps through the tunnel. I did, still nothing. I finally resolved that my bike had been stolen.

I walked up stairs in the station to the café with the Internet that I had searched so hard to find days earlier. I wrote another e-mail to my Dad, used Facebook, and logged into my E-trade account. From my E-trade account I had a message labeled, Urgent!

The message disclosed that unusual trading activity had taken place from my account. I was to call them immediately. The balance was now zero and it had been well over fifteen thousand dollars. I was dumbfounded. I had been in Madrid for three days doing everything in my power to prevent myself from being robbed by being responsible. All the while two events completely beyond my control robbed me blind.

I completed my Internet session determined not to let these events ruin my trip. I left the computer lab with E-trade's phone number in hand. I would ask Liisa when I got to Tilburg what was the easiest way to call the E-Trade.

I continued to ponder. Had someone watched me type my password in one of the Madrid Internet cafes? Was the crying lady just a distraction? Maybe there was keyboard stroke recorder, or was the connection secure? I wondered if this meant I should now change my Facebook, e-mail, and banking passwords?

I have enough money to last me for the rest of trip. I put the thoughts of the thefts to the back of my mind. Then I went to the kiosk to purchase my train ticket to Tilburg. It was now 1:00 p.m. I needed to meet Liisa at 5:00 p.m. The one positive was that I did not have to carry the fold up bicycle on the train.

The Dutch countryside rolled by my train window. I imagined a masked criminal riding into the sunset on my fold-up cruiser only to have the left pedal break free as he attempted to beat a delivery truck through a crosswalk. Then I reminisced on the good will that had surrounded that bike since it entered the Netherlands. Finally, I reasoned that this was my payback for stealing Celine's bike from Watersley years ago.

My ticket was to West Tilburg, where the University of Tilburg was. I had plans to explore Tilburg while I waited on Liisa to get out of class. The train came to Tilburg Central. I got off. I walked to the tourist information office and asked for information. She gave me a book in Dutch, a book in English, and a map of the entire town. I asked to use her table to plan my route. She happily told me I could.

I left shortly after and began to trek my way around town. It was modern yet old, just like many of the Dutch towns. Rotterdam was the most modern Dutch city I had seen, because I had read it was fully bombed out by the Nazis. Amsterdam, on the other hand, seemed quite ancient because with most bombings it was spared. Tilburg, I devised stood somewhere in the middle. I snapped pictures of churches, fountains, and parks. Then I had a good sit on a park bench. It was now 3:30 p.m. and I walked back to the train station and caught the next train to West Tilburg.

I got out of the train and pulled out my info for Liisa's apartment. Hoogscholan was the road I was looking for. The street number was 136-01. I located the exact address on the train station map and began to walk towards the school's campus. I could see what looked like a university center and decided to borrow their bathroom. I entered and used their facilities. I made my way out into the courtyard. College kids were walking, biking, and running to make it to classes that started ten minutes ago.

I walked across the campus and took a left. I had no map other than the picture in my mind of the map at the train station. I went left and walked down and alley. The name Hoogscholan was on the street sign. I had found it. There was a building that looked like dorms. It was not 4:30 p.m. yet. I decided to post up outside the complex after verifying the building contained the 136-01 room number she provided me.

I sat at the intersection of Hoogscholan and the university sidewalk. I imagined she was in class and would be coming from that direction. Thirty minutes passed. Out of the corner of my eye, I noticed her. It had been over four years since Watersley. She was still easily recognizable. I walked up and hugged her. I felt a relief. She asked if my backpack was all I had. I knodded, yes. Then I told her that I had one more bag but it was taken from me along with my bicycle. I decide to tone down the bad news for now and ask her about her friend Eeva who had also lived at Watersley. She would arrive in Tilburg next Thursday. Then we spoke about her class and her roommates. She said she had a group meeting in the common area of her dorm at 5:30 p.m. We walked upstairs, and I sat my bag down in her room.

    I then walked to the common area. I met a large majority of her classmates. There was another Finish girl, a German girl, and a Brazilian girl. I listened to their class meeting for graduate school and asked Liisa if she had Skype. I wanted to get my E-Trade situation under control. She said she had Skype. I would have to add money to her account. This was no problem, and I went to her room and logged in. I added money with my credit card and was able to call the United States for less than two cents per minute.

    I talked to the representative for fifteen minutes and completed multiple challenges to insure my identity. The multiple-choice questions the agent gave me were difficult. The questions were tough. I knew I had probably missed at least two by the end of the pop-quiz. I could not remember the amount of my mortgage, or my college PO Box number.

I was informed I had failed, and was put on hold.

    A supervisor picked up two minutes later and the connection was weak. I called back two minutes later and got put on hold. An operator came on with another set of challenges. She had an additional supervisor on the line. They gave me a three way phone grilling. Luckily, these questions were easier. I got each one correct. They could finally tell me what was going on. Someone had traded all my shares and moved my money to an offshore account. E-Trade agreed to reverse my positions to one day before the fraudulent trade had occurred. I went back to the living room with the weight of missing fifteen thousand dollars off my shoulders.

    Liisa had decided we would cook Mexican food. We left the common area and went across the street to the Albert Heijn and bought groceries. My selections were ground beef, tortillas, taco seasoning, strawberry juice, cheese, bread, beer, and chips. We arrived back at the dorms and began to cook. I had my first actual beer since Halloween in Amsterdam. We ate burritos for dinner and socialized with her other roommates. All total there were nine.

    Nina was a Brazilian student. She felt sorry for me having my bike stolen, and she had a bike that I could borrow. This would be a full sized Dutch bike instead of my missing fold up model. We finished out the night watching television in the living room. I offered Nicko a beer, and he accepted. He grabbed one and took a sip. Then he spit a mist into the air. He must not have liked it, I guessed.

"This is Amstel non-alcoholic," he said.

One of the six packs of beer that I had purchased was non-alcoholic. I just picked by the label color at the store. I offered him one of the full strength Jupilers. We joked how these Amstel beers would be there for the rest of the semester and beyond. Then I went into Liisa's room, and I filled my air mattress. It had been a long day since the 4:00 a.m. beginning in Madrid.

5th November, 2009
2:14 a.m.

Today I slept till around noon. Liisa checked her e-mail and her classes were cancelled. This was a common occurrence. This also meant the weekend started now. She did have doctor's appointment today. I decided I would go to town with her on the bus. I could walk around while she was at the doctor's office. Then we would meet up and look for Halloween costumes.

Liisa was a social chairman at her school and she had planned an after Halloween, Halloween party. It was at a local bar in two days. I had an 11:00 a.m. flight to Pescara, Italy on the day after this party. All indications were that everyone in the dorm building stayed up until 6:00 a.m. on weekend nights. After her appointment, we met back up the town center and went to several shops.

Once we arrived back at the flat there was a note at the door that another floor was hosting a DJ party. It was 10 euros for entry. The admission included free drinks and music. We had just purchased ours beverages at the store so Liisa asked if we could bring our own drinks and not pay a cover. They said yes.

We arrived at the party and the group was primarily Dutch students. They had removed the couch from the common area and leaned it on the railing of the balcony, upright. I counted one hundred and twenty full cases of Bavaria beer stacked up in the apartment and on the porch. There was only a four-foot area left for standing. In the kitchen area was a DJ who played decent Top 40, Techno, House, and Electronic music.

I was soon involved in a team chugging contest. A South African, a German, and I were up against the three Dutch guys who lived in this apartment. They poured us of Bavaria beer into glass cups. We all prepared and grabbed our glasses.

An arbitrary Dutch party girl came out of nowhere and said, "Go!"

Our team made it to the third cup on our side and the Dutch team called a false start. It was their apartment, so we played by the house rules. We re-poured and the anticipation built.

The Dutch girl walked in once more from behind the hallway, and yelled, "Go!"

Our number one man drank his with lightning speed. The Dutch team's first drinker was just creeping along. We were halfway done with our number two when they started on theirs. Then the number two drinker on our team finished, and it came to me. I turned the cup straight up and swallowed twice. We beat them by a full cup, as their third player never even got to start.

5th November, 2009
11:00 p.m.

This morning I woke up and I had breakfast with Nina in the kitchen. She handed me a key to her spare bicycle. Then she walked down with me and showed me where it was. As we unlocked it from six deadbolts, chains, wheel locks, and bar bolts Nina held the door open for light. As the door was open Jason walked by. Someone at the party described him as, the crazy drunk dancing Asian. Actually, he was from South Africa. He did have an eastern look to him. He said he was going to the city center. I asked if I could follow him. He agreed and he waited on us to undo the chastity belt of bike chains.

I was now cruising at 15 mph on a bicycle highway through Tilburg. I followed Jason close behind. This was a true bicycle highway. The road had stoplights, turn lanes, and a full marked four lane roadway . We accelerated onto the on ramp pedaling heavily. I searched for a new gear. With two clicks of the thumb gear shift, I heard a crack. There was no torque in the pedals. The pedal arms were now spinning at an incredible rate. My legs began to slow. I did not lose a pedal this time, but I had dropped the chain.

I pulled into the emergency lane of the bike freeway and flipped the bike upside down on its seat and handlebars. I needed to get a better look. Jason made a U-turn at the appropriate turn around location and was heading back in my direction. He told me to mount the chain on the largest sprocket. This is what it took to achieve decent bike highway speed. I resolved to leave it in this one highway gear for the remainder of my bicycle career in Tilburg. This way I could avoid these circumstances in the future.

    We arrived in the city center after another ten minutes of riding. This was far faster and cheaper than taking either the train or a bus. I followed Jason to a store where he would buy printer ink. After this we parted ways, because he wanted to shop in a Chinese market and he was being weird about me tagging along. As he walked away I thought that he might be part Asian after all.

    I then walked through town thinking about what I would be for Halloween. I was given a second chance after not dressing as anything in Amsterdam. I did not want to mess it up. I looked around several shops and found nothing.

    I rounded up my bike from the racks. Then I headed back to the grocery store to buy dinner. I bought pasta and spaghetti sauce. I grabbed an eight pack of beer, and rode to the dorm. I parked and locked my bike on the rack outside the hall.

    Liisa was in her room when I got back and she introduced me to another American studying there, Fred. He was studying abroad, from Chicago, and doing his entire degree in the Netherlands. This was his senior year and he would graduate in May. I went with him into the city center that evening and he gave me a local's tour of the best places to go in Tilburg.

6th November, 2009
11:45 p.m.

    I just came home from the city center. I was at Liisa's University Halloween party. I had no costume, but one of the girls had a stethoscope so I just put it around my neck and acted like I was doctor. I checked a few heartbeats with my stethoscope and told the girls to take a few shots of Jager and call me in the morning. I left the party on Nina's bike. Then I rode back to the room so that I could make it Eindhoven in the morning for my flight to Pescara, Italy. I will be there for four days and I have a host who will pick me up at the airport around noon.

7th November, 2009
11:45 p.m.

    I rolled out of bed and made my way to the bathroom. I packed some final things and headed to Tilburg's train station. I took the train all the way to Eindhoven, and bought a bus ticket to the airport. I hopped on bus 401 just like I did a few days earlier.
    The flight was smooth and the Alps were awesome from above. I now waited outside of the airport in Pescara, Italy for my Couchsurfing host. I knew that her name was Vanessa, and this was all the information I had. What she knew about me was similar. Flight after flight arrived. I watched people hug their long awaited friends and relatives.
    I watched the clock for over an hour. I knew nothing about Pescara. I had no phone card or any information about the area. I

stared at the clock as it taunted me. I noticed a girl reading brochures by the rental car booth.

I walked over to her and timidly said, "Vanessa?"

It was her. I hopped in her car, and we went to her apartment. She showed me my private room and bathroom. Vanessa prepared me an Italian coffee as I sat at her bar and we got acquainted. We then took a walk on the beach. It was right across the street from her apartment. I snapped photos and asked her a plethora of questions about the local area.

I arrived back at her place around 6:00 p.m. I asked to use the Internet. I sent out a few e-mails and then the doorbell rang. It was Dominicko. He was Vanessa's boyfriend. They began talking rampant Italian. I understood nothing. I logged off the computer just as they offered me special beer that had a smoked flavor. It was delicious bacon beer.

They then told me about a wine harvest festival. We would drive to a nearby village. I could sample fresh regional dishes and try their finest 2009 batch of wines. We made our way down the flights of stairs. I got into Dominicko's Honda. Anything I had heard about Italian drivers was true. He pulled out in front of traffic and went twice as fast as the speed limit. For some reason, I did not care. I had prepared myself for this reality beforehand. I reminded myself of the few times I rode in a car with a foreign driver. I did this before I ever buckled my seat belt. To prove how comfortable I was, I went to sleep.

I awoke as we pulled up a stone driveway. We got out of the car. I had no clue if they had been giving me details about the area, or how long I had slept. They might have been asking me questions too. I was oblivious. I got out of the car and followed them into a building.

We went up five flights of stairs and into an apartment. They introduced me to two more people. Their names were Anna and Carlo. We walked back down the stairs. The group proceeded to get into Carlo's car. He was driving. He was a mountain climber and preferred to be dropped from helicopters on the highest peaks of the Alps. I took this to mean his driving style might be a bit risky too. I sat in the back with Dominico. Anna sat on the hump. Vanessa was up front with Carlo.

We sped onto the highway. He squealed around corners too big for two cars to pass. It seemed like we were rolling on two wheels. Then we entered a forest road lined with trees. After a hairpin turn, we began climbing a mountain.

Vanessa asked, "Are you doing O.K.?"

I told her, "I am doing fine. We have similar roads in Tennessee."

She said, "Yes, but not similar drivers."

I decided to once again show them my comfort level with their driving and I went to sleep.

I awoke as we pulled off the road and behind a line of cars edging a stone laden cliff. We exited the car and entered the town. I was given facts about the festival, the homemade foods, and the area. We ate soup with bits of lamb. I spat occasionally to jettison a sheep bone that had made its way into my mouth.

I listened to a band and ate soup while I drank fresh wine. I relished the awesomeness of the moment. I tried to pay. Nobody in the group would let me. They bought two of everything and gave me one of the full portions. I ate fried pizza, porquette, bread, pasta, fries, and roasted nuts. I had the feeling that they had read somewhere that Americans like to eat. I was stuffed.

I was enjoying my wine as the temperature dropped. It was now freezing and my only defense from the cold was wine. Eventually, the rest of the group was cold and we went back to the car. I watched a few hairpin curves go by, and then I went to sleep. I woke up at Carlo and Anna's flat. I got out of the car and moved over to Vanessa and Dominicko's car. I fell asleep once more on the way back to their apartment. I awoke as we pulled into their driveway.

8th November, 2009
10:45 p.m.

I arose this morning and Vanessa and Dominicko were just getting out of bed too. They made breakfast. Then they informed me me we would be going to the mountains today. I needed to dress warm. We filled water bottles and loaded the car. We drove out of town and into the mountains. I fell asleep once more.

"Get out and take a picture!" Vanessa said as she socked me in the arm from the front passenger seat.

I woke up, took a picture, and got back in the car. Then I fell asleep. When I awoke once more we were at a field. We got out of the car and started walking on a trail. We walked three miles before coming to a set of steps. We went downhill and found a wooden door. This was a commune that people would come and live in. They stayed here when they needed to re-connect with God. On the inside there was a communion table. The table had wine, bread, and a Crown Royal tin. There was a hole punched in the top for offerings.

 We exited out the back door of the commune. Then we came to another set of steps. This time there was no wall beside of them. It was a 300-foot drop. We carefully descended down the rock face until we were in a valley. There was a riverbed at the bottom, but no river. It was dry. I read a placard about the native amphibians that was surprisingly in English.

 Then we made our way back to the car where a Shepard and his sheep dog greeted us. I fed the dog my left over fried pizza from the festival last night. We got in the car once more and drove to a mountain spring. We refilled our water bottles. It was delicious and really quenched my thirst. I always liked to drink water wherever I go because I felt like the bacteria would strengthen my immune system on my future endeavors. My theory is that after our bodies ingest water in any country, town, or state we develop immunity to it in the future. This could prove very helpful for me if water sanitation systems should ever fail. As I thought about my iron gut, I fell asleep.

 My eyes opened once more as we pulled into a mountain ski lodge. It was too cold for a hike. I rejoiced silently. It was 30 degrees cooler outside the car than when we had gotten in at Vanessa's apartment. She lives near the beach, and we are on the mountain. We walked inside the lodge to grab a beer and snacks.

After our third bag of chips and a beer we got back in the car. I fell asleep again and woke up as we pulled into a side street of another unfamiliar Italian town. We walked up the street and entered a building. I met four people and had another glass of wine. They told me that George Clooney was filming a movie locally called, "The American." They walked me up the street and showed me the flat he owned. I suppose when it is released I will know if they were telling me the truth or not.

It was now 8:30 p.m. We were preparing to cook dinner. Dominicko was making homemade pasta. I asked if I could take a lesson. We took three eggs, a pile of formia, a wooden cutting board, and a rolling pin. We began to knead the eggs and formia together. After five minutes we had the noodle dough formed into eight equal slices. I rolled them flat. Then I placed it on a box with strings called a guitar. It was used to cut the noodles. We placed them in a pot of boiling water and they softened very quickly. We ate these fresh noodles with salami, pepperoni, bread, gorgonzola, pecans, fresh olives, and wine.

We said goodnight and Vanessa told me that Dominicko had to work in the morning. She had a doctor's appointment, and she thought I should sleep in. Once she arrived home she would give me a tour of Pescara.

9th November, 2009
11:15 PM

Today was my last full day in Italy. I rode a bicycle down the beach in Pescara and explored. Then I met Vanessa and Domenicko in town and bought them lunch at a pizzeria they recommended. After this, Vanessa took me to a shop. I bought a coffee maker like hers. I am going to take it back with me to the United States. This afternoon I went with Domenico to a gym where he teaches rock climbing. His group travels to the Alps to climb, as these are the mountains are closest to them.

Although rock climbing is not my thing, because of a fear of heights, I gave it a shot. The one problem I ran into is that there is not an Italian man at the gym with a shoe that is larger than size six. I wear a size twelve. It is real punishment having to put on a shoe six sizes to small. For me to attempt a climb, I had to fight through the pain. My entire foot was curled in a downwards-arch shape, which actually gripped the crags on the wall very efficiently. The problem came when I left the wall and landed on the mats. The landings almost broke my poor feet. It was great exercise and a lot of fun. I was also glad when it was finished. I could now take my reverse curl elf shoes off.

I had a fantastic trip and stay with Domenicko and Vanessa. This is a very beautiful area. In the right season, I could surf in the morning at the beach, and then take a thirty-minute drive into the mountains and snowboard in the afternoon.

11th November, 2009
11:05 PM

I arrived back in the Netherlands safely yesterday, and today I went to Maastricht for the carnival that I have attended in 2004 and 2008. This year the security was much more visible and pushy. I am certain they have ruined it for everyone. I stayed for about 45 minutes as opposed to the typical full day event. I am back in Tilburg now and have three more days left. I was planning to go to Amsterdam on the last night, but Liisa said that I should just stay in Tilburg and catch a train that morning. So that is what I will do.

13th November, 2009
11:15 PM

Yesterday I toured the Tilburg Nature museum much to my delight. Today Eeva flew into Tilburg. She is Liisa's Finnish friend, and we all lived together at Watersley years ago. Eeva is currently working in China, and she arrived early this morning. While Liisa was at class we went to the Dutch town of Breda by train. While we were there we walked around shops and found several cafes to drink coffee and beer. We spent our time catching up on life over the past five years. Then we bought Burger King at the train station and brought it back to Liisa for dinner.

15th November, 2009
10:30 PM

Yesterday, we went into the city center of Tilburg early. By noon Liisa, Eeva, and I were yelling, clapping, and laughing out loud while enjoying spirits and each other's company. After our booze brunch reunion, we went shopping. I bought a pair of shoes, a poster, and a few smaller items to give away. We came back to the apartment after our trip down to the center and I began to pack my bags to leave for Amsterdam tomorrow morning. It was a pleasure to get to see Liisa and Eeva as they have always made me feel at home even when we lived at Watersley. I made it to Amsterdam fine and flew out this morning and just made it back to my couch in Dandridge, Tennessee.

22nd December, 2009
12:30 p.m.

I am sitting at the office and thinking about what to get my mother for Christmas. When I left for Amsterdam a few months ago I kissed her goodbye.
The last thing she said to me was, "The next time you go to Europe, take me with you."
    I told her, "I would."
    My plan now is to give Mom a card that has a dozen European cities listed. Then I will let her choose which cities she wants to see. If distance is an issue, I can find a similar city. It will be interesting to see where she chooses.

19th May, 2010
1:45 p.m.

My mother was impressed with her Christmas gift. She recently made her final decision on cities. The cities she wanted to see where Rome, Paris, and Cinque Terre. I finalized a flight and have started working on the rest of the details. I booked two roundtrip tickets to Brussels. For her birthday, which is on the 21st of May, I will purchase a rental car for our trip. I am also booking hotel rooms since the exchange rate is favorable now. I just purchased a hotel room in Brussels for the last night of our trip. The official dates of my next journey are October 22nd through October 30th.

From the travel journal of Barbara Leonard

My First Trip to Europe

22ⁿᵈ October, 2010
7:00 p.m.

    My son Jobe who gave me this trip for Christmas 2009 came to the house at 7:00 a.m. and we had a French toast breakfast to start the day off with some grease. The extra piece went to my dogs, Jamocha and Poco, to split. I finished my morning groom, and darling David came home from work to take Jobe and I to the Knoxville airport. We left here around 10:00 a.m. and arrived in plenty of time for our flight to O'Hare in Chicago. I have not been to Illinois in over three years. We will only be at the airport, but Illinois is still my home state.
    There was a couple hour layover before we board to Brussels, and I found a lucky penny at the Knoxville's McGhee Tyson airport

right off the bat. I am really excited and pumped for this trip. I am packed and organized. I slept well last night. My boy, Jobe and me, we are heading across the pond.

22nd October, 2010
7:00 p.m.

    It is now around 7:00 p.m. We are officially leaving O'Hare. We had a delay and were forced to change planes due to mechanical problems. Our takeoff was supposed to be at 4:45 p.m. We had a lunch at McDonald's in O'Hare at around 1:00 p.m. I hope to eat soon after we take off for Brussels.
    They pulled this plane out of the hanger. It still smells like mothballs. I hope this baby can fly. It is a full jumbo jet. We are seated in the back few rows, close to the bathrooms. We will be on the plane for eight and a half hours.

23rd October, 2010
10:00 a.m.

    We landed in Brussels. Our plane flew over here all night long. We had supper on the plane. Then I slept off and on. Coach was crowded and uncomfortable. Jobe and I did sleep. I ate breakfast on the plane when the sun was coming up. Then we landed in Brussels. At the airport we picked up our rental car, a Mercedes Benz. We are off and heading to our first destination Milan, Italy.

23rd October, 2010
11:00 p.m.

We drove through Belgium and right into Luxemburg. It was a small country so it was not long before we made it into France. This took us about four hours. We stopped for gas and snacks. There were no side trips today as we are headed for Milan. We need to make our hotel reservation there. We lost a few hours with the plane delay last night. We were in France today for three hours or so and then we drove into Switzerland. I knew we were getting close when I started seeing the Swiss snow covered Alps in the distance. We are headed right for them.

As we drove into Switzerland the customs agents at the border asked for our passports. They wanted to know what we were doing. They were very friendly. We told them we were on a holiday. Jobe rolled the window up, and off we went. In Switzerland it was colder and windy. It had been a clear nice day all day and probably around 50-60 degrees Fahrenheit. We drove through many tunnels. The longest tunnel through a mountain was eleven miles as we passed through the Alps.

Then as it was getting dark we were right at a huge snow covered mountain. We witnessed the most beautiful sight. We sped down the Swiss highway and a full moon was coming up just behind a mountain peak. It was shining down on Lake Cuomo. Jobe said it looked surreal, and it did. It was really something with the moon's reflection on the lake surrounded by the snow-covered Alps.

STUDY ABROAD

When we neared the southern border of Switzerland we were approaching Italy. The tunnels through mountains were becoming less frequent. We listened to the radio. Jobe also brought CD's on basic Italian and French vocabulary. We practiced aloud in the car. It was fun. Finally, we drove into northern Italy and then another forty-five minutes took us into Milan.

It was now nighttime. Jobe's GPS took us through the center of the city. Then we pulled right up to our hotel in the inner city of Milan. It was a Holiday Inn, and boy was it good to get out of the car. We parked in a garage across the street from our hotel. Our room was number 222.

We were both hungry and tired so Jobe took a look outside our hotel window. Without saying a word he walked out the door. When he came back five minutes later he had a pizza pie. It was brick oven baked with Gorgonzola cheese. He also had two Cokes. We ate our first Italian meal. It was an authentic Italian pizza in our room. It was delicious.

We were in bed shortly after, around 10:30 p.m. It felt so good to lie down after a nine-hour flight and an eleven-hour drive. The temperature was perfect without even adjusting the air. After being on a plane all night and in a sitting position we were in heaven lying in our beds all stretched out. Jobe did all the driving. I suppose he was really whipped. We were in five countries today. We really made tracks. Our destination for tomorrow is Rome. We are touring Milan in the morning. Good night.

24th October, 2010
11:00 a.m.

We woke up early. Jobe, a bird, like his Dad, got up first and went to the lobby to get on the Internet. He e-mailed his Dad that we arrived and checked the news. He found out that Tennessee got beat by Alabama, 41-10. I showered and dressed. Jobe brought me a cup of coffee. It was like a thimble. Jobe says that there is no such thing as American drip coffee in Europe. It was small, but tasty.

Then we were off to catch a streetcar. We went to see The Cathedral Duomo and Milan's city center. It was 8:00 a.m. There was not much going on, but the streetcar was full. We got a good look at the stores, buildings, ancient architecture, and European flavor of Milan. The buildings were magnificent and there were balconies off almost all the windows. Many of them had flowers and vines.

It was a cloudy day and almost misting. I took pictures and walked around the cathedral plaza. The pink marble of this beautiful magnificent cathedral is hard to describe. The big wooden double thirty foot high doors were all hand carved. There were all kinds of saints and biblical scenes sculpted all around the cathedral from top to bottom.

We hopped back on the streetcar and got off to find breakfast. I located a café named Bar Barbara. We took a picture. We did not eat there. It was only a café with sweet rolls.

We walked to a grocery store and got sandwich food, fresh cheese, pesto, a bag of cookies, and a fresh baguette. Then we got on the streetcar once more and went back to our hotel. Once there we made sandwiches, and a few for the road.

**24th October, 2010
11:00 a.m.**

    I am back in the car now. Our destination today is Rome. Something that I experienced in Milan was a roundabout. They are everywhere. It is a circle drive that replaces a stoplight or stop sign. It has four or five exits with streets coming off of the perimeter. I also noticed working class people mixed with fancy dressers on the streetcar. Public transportation was a great way to go slow and look at the city back and forth. I am still trying to get it through my head that I woke up today in Milan, Italy.

**24th October, 2010
9:00 p.m.**

    It was a four-hour drive to Rome. The weather got better as we closed in on Rome. Instead of finding our hotel, we got lost. We accidentally drove into downtown Rome. We were in the very heart of Rome. Jobe drove around, and around, and around once more.
    We drove right by the Vatican City. All the streets had many sculptures of angels and horses. The beautiful gigantic sculptures and architecture were everywhere we looked.

Everyone was driving crazy. Motorbikes weaved in and out of the lanes of cars. Horns were beeping, and cars were pulling out in front of us. Jobe handled our Mercedes like a pro. He blasted through the dusty streets with our manual transmission like he had lived in Rome all his life. We got lost, but we were able to see so much of the inner city in old Rome. Then quite by accident we drove up a narrow windy road to the top of a hill. It was a park and a wall with flowers. There was a large horse sculpture that was at least three stories high. I overlooked the wall. I could see the entire city of Rome. We took lots of pictures here.

Then we used the GPS to guide us to our hotel. We probably drove around Rome for three hours total. We arrived at our hotel and Jobe had booked another Holiday Inn. We had a nice room with two beds and I am writing from one of them. We opened the window, and there is a nice breeze blowing in.

After settling in, we walked down the hill to find supper. There was not much around so Jobe told me he really enjoyed eating at McDonald's while overseas. We grabbed a burger and fries and it was delicious. Then we walked to the grocery store and got a few things including beer, pop, and more sandwich meat.

We walked back to the hotel and Jobe had a beer as he worked on our plan for the Vatican and Sistine Chapel tomorrow morning. Then we walked again for an evening walk in the dark. It felt really nice to stretch my legs after being in the car. As we walked I recalled last Sunday night when I talked with Jobe on the phone in Dandridge.

I asked Jobe where we would be next Sunday night.

He said, "Rome, Mom," and here we are.

Our plan for tomorrow morning is to take the metro to the Vatican City and get up early. We want to arrive early so we do not have to wait in a long line. My dream come true is to see the Sistine chapel with my own eyes. I will go to bed by 10:30 p.m. and get up early at 6:30 a.m. and then go, go, go.

**25th October, 2010
10:30 p.m.**

Today I was up at 6:30 a.m. and ready fast. We were out the door by 6:50 a.m. We beat four to five big tour busses out of the parking lot and went to town. We drove to a side street in Rome that was six or seven blocks away from a metro station. It was the last metro on the line. We were on the outskirts of Rome.

We rode this metro to the stop right next to the Vatican. Then we walked eight more blocks to the Vatican wall. There was already a long line. It was beginning to rain. My umbrella and rain jacket were in the car. When it became a full on rain shower I bought a five-euro umbrella from a street vendor working the line of people waiting to enter. We got in line at 8:30 a.m. Jobe and I made it into the museum at around 10:30 a.m. Jobe knew we would have to wait. It is closed Sunday and open on Monday at 9:00 a.m. Even getting in line thirty minutes early for the Vatican opening is an hour late. It was worth every minute of waiting, times ten.

I had no idea what was inside the Vatican. I only really knew about the Sistine Chapel. Jobe knew what was there because he had been to the Vatican several years ago when he was a student in the Netherlands at international business school. I really do not know how to put in words what it was like being inside the Vatican City walls. Overwhelming, the exquisite ancient preserved beauty of the buildings courtyards, walls, stairs, and all the many rooms.

Jobe took a video of everything so if one ever had the chance to watch it would be worth seeing what I have just witnessed. We started in a courtyard and walked into a hallway of head busts of famous Roman rulers, emperors, and big marble sculptures. Then another room of beautiful sculptures of animals big and small. Next we came to a room of more sculptures, a courtyard of urns, statues, and marble tubs that were used for Baptisms.

Next we were on to another room full of more sculptures that were large, life-sized, or even larger. The Immaculate Conception painting followed this and room full of art depicting Mother Mary of God. These were the finest of artwork, sculptures, and paintings on humongous canvases.

One particular big white marble sculpture really caught my attention. I took close ups of two cherubs who were part of the sculpture. It was allegorical. I loved the expressions of the two cherubs. From many of the windows, which were huge, I could see the city of Rome. I took a few pictures looking down upon it.

After this we traversed into a large room. It was a hall of giant tapestries of holy scenes. The windows were all blacked out to keep the sun away from the precious tapestries. In addition, to take my breath way, the ceilings were ornate and gothic. They had renaissance painted scenes and carved marble columns. Everywhere I looked for the entire visit was another stunning, beautiful, work of art. Unbelievable really, and it was so much more than I ever imagined. The most interesting, beautiful museum I had ever been in. Of course, being raised a Roman Catholic put plenty of special meaning to most of the religious artifacts and scenes that were portrayed.

I could easily see how rich and powerful the Catholic Church had been in Rome and all of Italy. They had the money to commission the finest and best artists, sculptors, and painters of the day to produce for the Vatican. They accumulated their masterpieces for hundreds of years and were able to keep an preserve it in pristine condition. It is really beyond comprehension. At times I felt like I was so close to the saints, angels, and God himself. One could close their eyes in many of the rooms and tell it is a Holy, Sacred place. To just know I was walking in the same footsteps as Popes, famous artists, kings, and queens was extremely humbling.

After all the rooms, the tour ultimately leads to the Sistine chapel or the Chappella Sistina. I felt like I needed to fall on my knees as soon as I walked in. A Swiss guard asked for silence. We walked in to the crowd of people inside and the soldiers reminded us that it was a sacred place. It was Stunning and beyond the beyond. I wanted to lay on the floor with my Wal-Mart binoculars and study the ceiling for a couple of hours. Instead I bent my neck and looked for thirty minutes. I used both my naked eye and my binoculars.

    I especially zoned in on God giving life to Adam, studying facial expressions where their fingers touch. It is in the center of the ceiling. I had to stand facing the altar to see it from a Mass attendee's point of view. It is a chapel and it is not like being in a big church, but very intimate really. There is a large Jesus on the cross and a Crucifix on the altar that looked almost ten feet tall. It was made from wood. I need to do research and study more about this famous chapel now that I have been here.

    I know the story of, Agony and the Ecstasy. Michelangelo painted the ceiling for the Pope who commissioned him. I have also heard of the disagreements they had. As I recall, the Pope was mad because Michelangelo was so slow and painted with such detail he was taking a long time and now everyone must be so glad that he did take his time. A ceiling for the ages, like no other. I am at a loss to describe what it felt like being in this chapel. Mostly I stared and looked at all aspects of the ceiling. Then I would sit for five minutes on the marble benches around the sides and then the benches against the walls. There were lots of people all sitting and standing all in sacred awe. I thought about how my Aunt Karen Booker would love this. I made the sign of the cross and prayed for my family, traveling mercies, and of thanks for this journey to such a sacred place. It was the true Catholic Mecca.

    The Sistine Chapel was about the end of the visit and we walked through more halls of antique displays. There were incense pots carved from stone, holy coins, carvings, and a collection of all sizes of crucifixes made from wood, stone, marble, ivory. Then long hallways of what looked like Cardinal's lockers. They were elaborate and ornately painted with names on golden plates above each one, and I could see a tiny keyhole. It was about the same size of a vestment locker and they were on either side of long and wide hallways. There were two hundred lockers over the course of four separate hallways.

    There was also a room of modern Popes and several areas of modern religious artworks. This was my least favorite so we moved quickly on to more ancient Roman busts. I did not know who any of them were, nor had I ever heard of any of them. It did not do much for me. All white marble, all men, all heads, and all ancient historical figures that were not exactly from the church.

    Jobe and I left and were probably inside for only three hours total. Someone could easily spend two full days. It was fifteen euros to get in. The next time I go to Rome I will plan a trip to go on the last Sunday of the month, because it is free. Then I will go back on Monday so I can stay for two whole days and really take it all in. I just got a quick overview today, and it was enough to make me want more.

    We were now leaving the Vatican City and walking back to the metro. It stopped raining and we were back on the subway in no time. Jobe was in front of me and he said, "Boy these steps are slippery."

One second later I was sitting on them. I slid on the stairs going down to the metro. I caught myself, so I was not hurt. I only fell down three steps. I leaned back when I went into slip mode and braced myself with my hands. Then I busted my ass.

We had made it back to our rental car after our fifteen-minute walk. We were thankful our car did not get towed or booted. Jobe had researched the parking area and thought it was a good spot. He went to the hotel lobby early this morning and snatched an Italian paper to put on the dashboard. This way we would look more local. Jobe prayed at the Vatican that we might be given forgiveness for parking in this little neighborhood. His prayer was answered, and our car was fine.

Our GPS lady got us out of Rome and back on the motorway. We were both sweating by this time. Rome was very warm and now humid after the rain. We headed to our next destination Portofino, Italy. It is northwest of Rome about 270 miles and located on the coast on the Mediterranean Sea. We had a bed and breakfast reservation there for tonight.

We had a great scenic drive through many tunnels. They became more frequent as we got further north, near the mountains. We passed through Tuscany, Umbria, and Ligernia provinces. Each province was somewhat hilly with a lot of small villages atop the hills. All of them had a church steeple visible. A majority of the villages were centuries old. Italians loved the dusky gold color, shades of orange, and pink tiles for their roofs. There are plenty of grape vineyards and olive tree groves. The tiny little villages most up on top of hills and mountainsides make me want to drop in and see how they live.

We rode into a blue sky and then a small shower. We then spotted a huge double rainbow and could see both ends with a huge cloud in the middle.

Jobe kept saying, "What does it mean?"

I felt that it was just a good sign, and on we went to Portofino. We are not going to make it to Cinque Terre, but maybe next time. Jobe picked Portofino, because he says it will be a lot like Cinque Terre, but much easier to access via automobile.

We arrived in Portofino around 5:30 p.m. We started to look for our bed & breakfast. It was a place called Kasa de Kiwi. Our accommodations were located up a very narrow winding road up on the side of a huge hill. Our point of reference was when we go to an ancient church called Bascilicia De Fieschi. We had trouble finding Kasa de Kiwi so we turned around at the church a few times in search for number fifty-two street marker. After our third run up the hillside, we went right to it. It was a lovely house. The view of Portofino and the ocean below was to die for. The scene was right out of a storybook. I took pictures, but they would not do it justice. Our host's name was Jimmy. He was an Italian who described Portofino as the most beautiful place in the world.

We promptly let ourselves in our room. Then we locked ourselves out. While we waited for Jimmy to return we went into the village to find supper. We drove around and quickly realized many of the places were more seasonal summertime restaurants that had already closed for the winter. We ate at a quaint but busy pizzeria, and had a cute young blond waitress who did not speak a single word of English. I had spaghetti and Jobe ate a pizza. He shared with me but refused to eat my spaghetti. We both drank a bottle of beer and watched The Simpsons in Italian. A little boy and his father were eating next to us and he was about nine years old and giggled a lot. He was cute, and I could not understand a thing that they were saying to each other. We finished our food and headed back up to our accommodations.

Our host Jimmy brought us a complimentary glass of red wine and we sat on the veranda outside our room. I looked at the ocean and village lights below. We made it to bed around 10:30 p.m. We were both tired as it had been quite an eventful day. From sun up to sun down were on a fast track tour of Europe. Breakfast is scheduled at 9:30 a.m. Jobe fell asleep first and was out like a light. It did not take me long either.

26th October, 2010
10:25 p.m.

Jobe and I each took a shower around 8:30 a.m. I ate an aspirin after waking with a headache, damn it. We ate on the veranda with Joe and Tim who were a couple from England who were at the bed & breakfast as well. Joe was actually a female. She was a little stuffy. We talked to Tim more than Joe and he was delightful. He was a music professor in London who taught rock guitar. We had fun talking with him and comparing English versus American traits. We told him we were heading for France today. He told us that the only thing that ruins the beautiful country of France, was the French.

We finished our breakfast. Jobe left our host, Jimmy, an orange Tennessee zip up bottle coozie. He was surprised and happy. We told him about Tennessee and the color orange. The room we were in last night was called the orange room. It contained lots of orange décor. This was appropriate for us.

Then we loaded our bags into the car. We stopped to take pictures of the little church near the Casa de Kiwi. We were off once more like a rocket. My chauffeur Jobe David Leonard was now zipping along on the motorway headed northwest to Italy's border with France. We slowly left green hilly Italy. By 2:15 p.m. we were entered France. We were in the middle of the snow-covered Alps. In fact, after we got into France, we were so high up that there was plenty of snow all around us. The roads were clear. We crossed the Alps and made our way to Lyon, which was now only one hundred more miles away. It was a pretty day and the sky was blue.

We drove straight through Lyon and then forty-five minutes north to Sandrans. We stopped in a little town named Sanave' to use an ATM. We are now in beautiful flat farmland and countryside. It looks a lot like Illinois with all the corn, cows, and crops. The houses are all stucco with tile roofs.

We pulled into our next bed and breakfast in Sandrans, France at around 6:00 p.m. Dominique and Robert hosted us in a three hundred year old farmhouse. This location also doubled as a working Charolais cow farm. It had a lovely and old world feel. The bedroom and the bath were country style, but modern.

We put our bags down and walked around the town of Sandrans. The population was only 487 people. The town had the usual ancient church and stone cherub fountain. There was a monument for all the children that died during the influenza outbreak of 1914-1918. Autumn had brought out lots of colors everywhere. Many hardy flowers were still blooming. We walked a while and went back to our bed & breakfast.

After resting a minute, we got back into the car. We drove into the next village to eat supper. We found a nice restaurant and walked in. We were told, in French, that they did not open until 7:00 p.m. So we decided to explore this town a bit too. The charming name of the town was Chatilloon. It had many little shops that we walked around and visited. I bought post cards, and Jobe used the Internet at a computer repair shop. The nice young man let Jobe use his computer for one euro. He sent an e-mail to his father. We walked back outside into the chilly but clear evening. Both of us immediately zipped our jackets up.

The restaurant we found earlier, L'Okovango, was now open for business. We had a very delicious meal. I had brochettes de bouef and it consisted of beef, red peppers, sautéed zucchini, and was served in a black pot like a child's dish with wild rice. Jobe ordered a'bouef entrée as well and he loved it Carpaccio de Bouef an Parmesan. We also ate French fried potatoes, but not cut into the shape of a fry. They were in a more natural shape, of wedges, with the seasoned skin still on the outside. Everything was delicious and hot, including our basket of bread. Each of us scraped our plates clean. We were very hungry, because we did not eat lunch. After dinner we went back to Sandrans. Once again we were in bed by 10:30 p.m.

**27th October, 2010
11:45 p.m.**

    We woke up at 7:00 a.m. We both took showers in a warm heated bathroom. It frosted outside last night. The morning was clear, cool, and beautiful. Dominique served breakfast at 8:30 a.m. We had our bags in the car already.

    We sat down at a farm table. My eyes lit up when I noticed the drip coffee pot full on the counter of the country kitchen. I had not had a large cup of American coffee since leaving the United States. At our place settings were big white cereal bowls, juice glasses, and spoons.

    Dominique came over to the table and started pouring coffee into my empty cereal bowl until it was full. Then she did the same to Jobe's bowl. I was not sure if I was supposed to drink from the bowl or sip it from my spoon. I asked Jobe and he was holding back a laugh. I picked up the bowl and looked at Dominique inquisitively.

She said, "Oui" and nodded yes.

I looked at Jobe again, and he was still grinning. I started drinking directly from the bowl. I was so damn glad to get a full cup of coffee I would have emptied it no matter what she poured it in. We had juice, toast, and a muffin by the warm heat of a wood stove burning red, with the morning's first fire.

After breakfast Dominique's husband Robert came into the kitchen and shuffled us out the door. Our breath could be seen outside. He motioned for us to follow him. He took us through a farm gate and showed us his prize cows, and all the trophies he had received over the past forty years. It was really impressive, and he had almost six shelves full of awards and plaques.

There were little calves. They were super cute. He also pointed out his champion bull. We chatted a minute out in the barn with Jobe and I using our limited French. They spoke only French and no English. We communicated. It was a very pleasant visit to the country village of Sandrans and a nice stay in a three hundred year old farmhouse.

We were on the road at 9:10 a.m. and driving towards Paris. Chauffeur Jobe decided we would take back country roads and highways for the scenery and to avoid a few tolls. It was a gorgeous day. We will be driving for about five hours to Paris. We will park outside of the city and ride a metro into Paris. This will be similar to what we did in Rome. Jobe says it is the best way to avoid the inner city traffic and parking dilemmas.

The entire week before our trip Jobe had monitored an international situation in France where the oil refinery workers had been on strike. During our entire trip through Europe, we had zero troubles filling up our car, and by today we were certain that the crisis was over.

    We continued towards Paris, and we had a quarter tank of fuel remaining. Jobe got off an exit to refuel. Every station at the exit was closed, out of fuel, and chained off. We got back on the road and exited at the next stop. We had the same luck. After stopping a third time, I could tell Jobe was getting nervous. He stated multiple times that we would soon be empty. It was now essential that we fill up immediately. He began drafting behind tractor trailer trucks just to get more mileage in hopes that we could find a station before we became stranded south of Paris, and had to wait hours or days until the refineries were up and running again.

    We neared an exit while riding about ten feet behind a big truck. Jobe spotted a station off the exit to the left and put on his blinker. We exited the road and drove to the station where we proceeded to wait in a line for fuel. This line was twelve cars deep and at least forty-five minutes long. We made it to the front of the line just as our empty light went into emergency blink mode. It was a close call. Jobe got out of the car, prepared the vehicle to accept fuel. He slid my credit card into the gas pump. The credit card reader was unable to read the credit card. He tried it multiple times. Then he walked over to the kiosk to talk to the attendant.

    He came back and sat in the driver's seat Jobe told me that our American credit cards would only work on the other gas pump. The line to that pump was long and growing. We would have to go all the way to the back of the line. Jobe started up the car and drove forward. Bang!

We heard an extremely loud noise and a whipping sound. At the same instant we both looked over our shoulder to see what had just happened. Suddenly, I realized that Jobe had forgotten to take the gas nozzle out of our car before pulling forward. He had ruined one of the only working gas pumps in France.

In addition to that, everyone who was in our line would now have to transfer over to the only remaining working pump at the station, including us. People in the cars started yelling at us in French. Jobe moved the car slowly backward. As he got out of the car once more, I noticed people smirking and others about to kill him. Jobe went back behind the car and began accessing the damage. The nozzle and hose for the pump were completely destroyed. Our car suffered a minor bend to the gas door.

Jobe leaned in the window and said to me, "They think I am a fucking idiot."

I started to belly laugh, because what else could I do. Funny is funny no matter where I am, and yes he kisses his mother with that mouth. We provided entertainment and amusement for those around us. We filled up at the only other pump with gas in France after another hour and a half. Then we made our way into Paris with a full tank of gas and a slightly dented gas door.

Jobe drove us right into the Paris. We found a parking garage that hooked up with Paris's inner city metro. He had chosen the last stop on the metro. We were in Paris, just not in the heart of downtown. That is where we were now headed. Our hotel was one block from the Eiffel tower, and near a metro stop. We parked in the garage. Then we each bought an all day metro pass and rode into town. We checked in our hotel around 5:00 p.m.

    I relaxed in bed for a half-hour. Jobe decided he would back track to the parking garage. He needed to retrieve his handheld video camera. He forgot the camera in the car. It was the size of a cell phone. He had been taking video of the entire trip. I took this time for relaxation while he re-boarded the bustling metro and rode back to the outskirts of town to get his camera from the car. On the way from our metro stop earlier, I had stopped in a place called Paul's bakery and bought a French pastry. I ate it while lying in bed. It was delicious. Maybe the best I have ever tasted. Magnifique!

    Once Jobe arrived back from getting his camera, we took off to the streets of Paris. Jobe had a map, plus he had been here before. He was my navigator for the entire trip. We walked first down to the Eiffel Tower. The desk clerk at our five star accommodations had informed us that the tower would light up on the hour, every hour. As we were approaching and looking in awe, it began. Wow! What a sight! We walked into the park surrounding the tower and sat on a bench. We watched people boarding the elevators and tramcars that provide rides to the top. There was a long line, and we chose not to do this.

    We had plenty of other sights to see in a limited amount of time. After the Eiffel Tower's light show finished, we boarded the metro with our all day tickets. We rode for free to the Champs Elysee'. We then walked through the highbrow downtown area of Paris.

"Gucci, Cartier, Louis Vitton" I read out loud off of the shops that lined the streets.

Jobe said, "You are beginning to sound like a rap song, Mom."

We stopped and stood on a bench to watch a few street dancers. They were putting on a show. From this vantage point, we were able to see them over the surrounding crowd. Four young men were break dancing. This is what I call no joints dancing. They were moving muscles and shaking their bones like they had no joints.

We kept walking and took the metro over to the Notre Dame Cathedral stop. We walked a little more. I knew we were close when we noticed the café Qausimoto. We also walked through what I imagined was the gay men's part of town. They were all standing together on the sidewalk waiting to get into bars holding hands. There were no women to be found. Finally, we made it to the cathedral. It was dark, because night had fallen. We got a fantastic look and many pictures. I also bought a postcard of the amazing cathedral.

Now it was time to walk alongside the Seine River. We waved from a bridge to a tour boat below. Fifty people waived back to us. We then took the metro once more using our day passes. In less than five minutes, we were at the Louvre. I had no idea it was so big. The Louvre wraps around about two city blocks. The walkway was domed elaborately with glass and steel. This led us into the courtyard. It was wide open and approximately three hundred yards long.

In the very middle was a gentleman playing the saxophone very soulfully. It was now about 10:30 p.m. We sat down on a concrete bench and had a cigarette while listening to the saxophone and watching the big fountain. My wandering imagination was being tickled by the music. It made me curious of what treasures and paintings were inside. I think I will return someday and spend an entire day at the Louvre.

After a sit and a good look, we were off. Our next stop on the metro was our hotel. We got off the metro, Jobe said we should grab a cold drink and go back to the Eiffel tower park. We could watch the 11:00 p.m. light show, and that is what we did. The glittering tower in Paris's night sky capped off our evening whirlwind tour of Paris.

We bought Eiffel tower key chains on the stroll back to our hotel. The street vendors were working overtime trying to get that one last tourist Euro, and they did. I am back at the hotel now. I will go to bed soon. Our room is very nice with two beds and plenty of room for both of us. I closed the shades and curtains tight so we might be able to sleep in a little.

28th October, 2010
11:45 p.m.

I stayed in bed until 9:30 a.m. When I awoke Jobe was gone. He came back in the door and told me when he woke up at 7:00 a.m. He began preparing his camera for the day. He realized his memory card was missing. He had already walked back to the

Eiffel Tower to the bench we sat on for the 11:00 p.m. light show. He found it right beside the bench. It was undisturbed at one of the most visited attractions in the world. This card was smaller than a dime. It was a really good move by Jobe to back track.

    I got out of bed and showered. I fixed two cups of instant coffee that was in our room. I was ready. Today we were going to northern France to visit a town called Amiens. We checked out, walked to the metro, and rode back to the garage where we parked our car on the outskirts of Paris. One could say that we blitzed Paris. We took in plenty in a short amount of time. My observations were that the Parisian women were all skinny and fashionable. They wore colorful eyewear, boots, tights, and skinny jeans. Scarves were very popular. I wore one the entire time like I was a native French woman.

    We are driving on the toll way again and the weather is beautiful once more. The only rain we had in any country was holy water from heaven. This came down on us while were standing in a two-hour line, waiting to get into the Vatican.

    We drove north and got lunch at McDonald's. We were waiting at the drive thru, and I witnessed a man drinking a beer. Jobe told me that it was common for McDonald's to sell beer in France. This makes it easy to have a beer with lunch in a plastic cup. We ate in the car and skipped the beer. We were anxious to get to Amiens so we could see the city. Jobe was excited to see Maxime. This was Jobe's friend he went to university with in Holland many years ago.

We arrived to Amiens around 1:45 p.m. This is a great town. I fell instantly in love with this French town and the Amiens Cathedral. Jobe drove me around the old French city for about fifteen minutes. He tried to find our hotel. We parked in a parking lot and walked till we found it. The hotel was on a street that was not reachable by car. I carried my overnight bag. Jobe had his backpack.

We found the Hotel Le Prieure. It is three buildings away from the famous Amiens, Notre Dame Cathedral. This is a stunning, atmospheric old hotel that has been an inn since the late 17th century. We checked in, and very quickly were up at our room. We climbed an old spiral wood staircase. We were staying in room 7. It was located at the top of the stairs. Our charming room had two beds and a wall of windows. The windows opened to the courtyard and a full second floor balcony. There were two long containers of red Geraniums still in bloom. The windows opened to the outside. I have not seen a screen yet in Europe. The windows connect me directly to the outside and the fresh air. I like it. We used the open windows to control the room temperature in our hotel rooms and did not touch a thermostat the entire trip.

After settling in, we were out walking the city in no time. I walked around the outside of the cathedral. This is the center of the town. We started looking for a Xerox office. This is where Jobe's friend Max works. We had trouble locating it and Jobe mistook a young man working in a copy shop as Max. Jobe told me to go up to him and try to prank him. I did. On the way over to Max's location, Jobe realized it was not him. It was too late. I went up to him and started asking ridiculous questions. I thought it was Max. I was expecting Jobe to come out from behind the corner. Jobe never showed up, and this young man looked at me like I was nuts.

    I walked back to Jobe. He pointed to a Xerox sign on the second level. We were close. Max's office was in the same building, just upstairs. A man opened the door after we buzzed the doorbell. We asked for Maxime. The man turned out to be Max's boss. He told Max he thought we were his family.

    Maxime was tall and slim. He was wearing a business suit, and he was happy to see his old friend, Jobe. He walked outside the office. We chatted and agreed he would come to our hotel around 6:30, after he got off work. We would find dinner and have a beer or two. Jobe and I went around town exploring and enjoying all the brick roads and shops. There were statues in the town square. Each intersection had a round about instead of stoplights.

    After we walked for a good while, we sat down at a sidewalk café and drank draft beer. We relaxed and people watched. It was a busy town with lots of children, high school age kids, and adults. The typical tourists we had seen in Rome and Paris were nowhere to be found. As I daydreamed, an older gentleman with gray hair and a younger woman came by. We had two chairs at our four-person table, I told them to sit down, in French. Jobe was inside refilling our beers.

    Jobe came back outside with drinks. He was surprised at my new friends. We all drank beer together for a better part of the afternoon. I talked in French from what I could remember from high school French class. I was able to carry on a conversation with the lady. The man jokingly told us that he was the King of Amiens. He did look semi-important in his distinguished suit. He stayed on his phone almost the entire time with different callers. Jobe said he was probably full of shit and full of himself. My observation was that the couple was not married. They were lovers just looking for a table where they could blend in and not stand out. We had plenty of fun interacting, visiting, and judging the locals.

    Next, Jobe and I stopped in a shop. After about thirty minutes of shopping, Jobe went back to the hotel. He left me in the clothing shop. I made it back to our hotel at 6:00 p.m. I had just enough time to freshen up for the evening. Jobe was hanging loose watching French television when I got back. After putting makeup on and styling my hair, we went down to the lobby to wait for Max.

    We left our hotel with Max and went to a bar. We sat in the sidewalk café seating. We sat out at a wine barrel table and had a couple more drinks. I started with a Vodka and tonic. After our drinks we walked again. Max took us to a great restaurant. The establishment was a fourth generation French restaurant. It was decorated with early 1900's era decorations.

    We walked upstairs and had a booth on the second level. We had great wines, and Max helped us order. I had the most delicious appetizer I have ever eaten. The ingredients were crab, ham, mushrooms, and spices all mixed together like a spread. Then it was placed in an oval dish. This was topped with cheese and baked. They served the dish piping hot. For my entrée I had broiled salmon. I ate homemade ice cream with raspberry sauce for dessert. We had a wonderful time laughing as we told stories. Jobe accidentally spilled his wine while telling an animated tale. It went across the table and on to Max's suit.

He jumped up and in a French accent yelled, "Oh! What a pity!"

I had the biggest laugh at his reaction, and Jobe apologized and ordered more wine. The food was the best meal we had in all our travels through Europe.

After dinner we walked to another bar. It was designed my Mr. Eiffel himself. It had been a bank, and was now a wine bar. It had plenty of character and was designed using heavy steel. We sat at the bar and chatted enjoyed a glass of wine and each other's company.

Then the men walked me to our hotel. It was a few blocks away. Max and Jobe went out to have time together on the town. Max had been a very gracious host, and friend. I hugged him goodbye. I also invited him to come to the United States and bring his girlfriend. Amiens is a splendid city and my favorite. No metro, a slower pace, and very beautiful city with a fantastic host.

29th October, 2010
5:30 p.m.

  We got up around 9:30 a.m. and showered. Jobe was already out and had gone to the car. He came back to the room with groceries including a fresh croissants, meat, cheese, and coffee. We ate in our room, on a cute table.
  We were ready to tour the Amiens Notre Dame cathedral. The Hotel of Prayer was our accommodations so we only had to walk three doors down to get there. Near the entry was a gift shop. I bought a book about the Amien's cathedral. The beautiful, magnificent building was constructed in the 1300's. We took a self-tour. This is France's largest and tallest cathedral. The Amien's cathedral could hold two of Paris's Notre Dame cathedrals inside of it. This building was unbelievable.
  I lit a candle in front of Jesus on the cross. I also prayed in front of the huge statue of the Virgin Mary on the kneeler. This ancient cathedral was so big. It was also easy to get in, and free. Our self-tour allowed us to look at each area and walk around as long as we wanted. I was particularly taken with a small chapel called The Sanctuary of Sacred Sacrament. There was also a cherub grieving with tears over the statue of a fallen comrade.
  We spent an hour looking and walking solemnly through this Holy cathedral. Yesterday Max informed us that when the Germans occupied Amiens they burned many of the buildings. This destroyed a large portion of Amiens. They left this cathedral alone, because it had a German cross. This

cross was displayed and painted onto a column in the middle of the church. He challenged us to look for it during our visit. We found it.

This was the finale of my cathedral tour. Jobe set it up. I had seen many fantastic cathedrals and churches. I started with Duomo in Milan. The Sistine Chapel in Rome followed. We then visited two smaller churches in Portofino and Sandrans. Then we visited the Notre Dame in Paris. I had ended my trip with a full tour of the Amien's Notre Dame. It has been very amazing to see all of these amazing cathedrals. The tour has been one of the largest thrills of my entire life.

Jobe had been to Europe four times before so I am not sure he was as moved. For a first time visitor, I have really taken in some great cathedrals in a short amount of time. I could not have dreamed up this trip in my wildest dream. I only knew that I wanted to visit France and Italy on my first trip to Europe. Now we have already been to six countries. Jobe has a brief tour of Holland planned for this afternoon before we head to Brussels to catch our flight home tomorrow.

We jumped back in our rental Mercedes and were off again. I really loved visiting Amiens. I hope to return one day to Amiens in the northern part of France. We are now headed for Maargraten, Netherlands. This is a side trip. Then we drive to Brussels to stay at a Marriott near the airport. Jobe has not told me much detail about this excursion. I am ready to notch one more country up on my belt.

Our drive from Amiens to Holland was very pleasant. Once again we are blessed with wonderful weather. This included blue skies, 60 degrees, and warm sunshine. The countryside rolls along from northern France and into Belgium. Then we drove into the Netherlands. Just as we entered into the Netherlands border, there were hoards of people on bicycles. It is mainly pastures and farmland. The country is filled with agricultural beauty that one typically does not think about when they daydream of Europe.

We see hundreds of semi trucks filled with potatoes on the motorway. Jobe said the Netherlands and the Dutch were big potatoes growers and eaters. He did have an issue with the way they served potatoes with globs of mayonnaise.

We made it to a very tiny town outside of Maastricht called Maargraten. We got out of the car. To my surprise we were at an American war cemetery. We walked and visited the entire hallowed grounds of the Netherlands American Cemetery and Memorial. This was primarily a WWII American soldier cemetery. When I realized how many graves were marked with white crosses, it made me sad enough to cry.

I just could not fathom how many graves there were. This is the largest military soldier cemetery, or any type of cemetery I have ever visited. Jobe told me had had visited before. When he arrived, they were about to close. He only got a peek and did not get the opportunity to walk through it. We arrived at around 3:00 p.m. The sun was shining through the trees. The graves were turning orange, gold, and red, in the sun's rays. We took a very somber walk.

There were over 8,300 American servicemen buried here from 1944 to early 1945. I told Jobe that the amount of tears that fell from the mothers' eyes back home, as a result of this place would be enough to fill a river. What sacrifices our American soldiers made.

We visited the onsite chapel. It might have been the smallest and most modest of all the cathedrals we had seen. It now held the most meaning and value. It was hard to imagine while praying, how hard the fighting must have been. Most of these boys were sent over here in their early twenties. This was the same age Jobe was, when I sent him to study abroad. These young men never got a chance to live their lives past their early twenties in the name of our freedom. We walked out of the chapel and rays of the sun were growing weaker. The sun was passed steadily behind the horizon. A single remaining ray of light beamed onto two adjacent graves. One was from Tennessee. The other was marked Illinois.

29th October, 2010
10:30 p.m.

We were now driving to our hotel in Brussels, Belgium. We arrived and checked into the Airport Marriott around 6:00 p.m. This was the last leg of my fabulous, exciting trip. Brussels was more American looking that the other places that we had been. We were near the airport. The hotel was the nicest yet. The space, the amenities, and the size of the beds were all first class. The bathroom was large and fully stocked with real washrags. This was pleasant. I had been using the same one to remove my mascara all week. I would wash it out, dry it, and re use it at each stop. Now I had a clean stack of washrags in my hotel room. I tossed my travel cloth in the trash. It was also the first hotel that had an ice machine. Jobe told me early and often, not to embarrass him by asking for ice in Europe. His favorite joke about ice is that Europeans forgot the recipe.

    We were now hungry after another full day of travel. We only had homemade sandwiches for lunch, and nothing else since breakfast in Amiens. We found a Domino's Pizza and settled on cheese pizza and a bottle of Sprite. We also tried to find a gas station to fill up our rental car. We had an early morning return. All the gas stations were closed at 6:00 p.m. I do mean all of them. It was reminiscent of our search for gas near Paris. Everything was closed, but not from the strike.

    We decided to hold off on that chore until the morning. We went back to the hotel for our final night pizza party. We watched and English news station on our hotel room T.V. I put on my nightgown and Jobe grabbed a bucket of ice. We enjoyed pizza and ice cold Sprite in our room, and it was delicious. I set the alarm for 6:30 a.m. We also got our bags packed and organized. I set out my outfit for the airport right down to the band aid I would need for my little toe. It is a sad night. This is our last night. I am road tired, but I could have traveled for a few more days. I loved every minute of it. I have a bit of sensory overload.

I am extremely thankful for good weather and safe passage. I am most thankful to my son Jobe who made this trip possible. He could be a professional tour guide and make a fantastic living. It would be impossible to create this trip or dream up the excursions, reservations, and routes he took us on. He drove the entire way. I calculated that we put 2,300 miles on our rental car's odometer.

30th October, 2010
10:45 a.m.

We were awake by 6:30 a.m. We jumped in our rental car and made our way to the airport. Checking in our flight was a drag. It was complete with long lines and lots of waiting. We finally boarded our jumbo jet around 10:00 a.m. We will arrive in Knoxville at 5:00 p.m. It is going to be a long day with one stop Chicago. I really get cramped riding coach and sitting so long in the rock solid seats.
"Our route is to fly over England, Ireland, and then into Canada before dipping down into Chicago near Lake Michigan," the pilot announces.
Jobe is by the window, and he is watching the three-hour video we made during the trip. I told him I wanted a copy for Christmas. That should be a much easier gift than this trip to Europe.

30th October, 2010
5:45 p.m.

    We pulled into our driveway in Dandridge, Tennessee about fifteen minutes ago. The family animals, Poco, Jamocha, and Little Kitty greeted us. They were very glad to see me. So was my honey David. He got a little lonely, I think. As much as I loved my European tour, it is great being home. There is no place like my home. My bed, my pillow, my blanket, my bathroom, my pets, and my husband David are all I need. David made me two big vodka and grapefruits per my request, and I hit the bed.

About the author

Jobe Leonard lives in Dandridge, Tennessee. He is a project manager with Hearthstone Homes and has currently built over 100 custom log and timber frame homes in 26 different states. This includes a recent project he managed that was named the 2012 National Log Home of the Year. In addition, he serves as the current CEO of the rapidly expanding Internet startup company LakeFun.com and also works a contributor and content creator for GoOverseas.com.

If you found this book enjoyable, an honest review on Amazon, Facebook, or Twitter would be appreciated. Also tell a friend and consider giving Study Abroad as a gift to a student, friend, or loved one. This is a heart felt work created over the past decade, and we hope you enjoyed it.

Easy ways to get involved

1. Leave a review on a bookseller's website.
2. Post on Twitter, Facebook, or your blog.
3. Ask a bookstore to stock Study Abroad.
4. Give Study Abroad as a gift.
5. Tell friends, family, and coworkers.

Helpful links: www.Jobe.ws
www.Facebook.com/StudyAbroadBook
www.Twitter.com/JobeLeonard

Other New Books by Jobe Leonard:
Log Home Package
Timber Frame Home Package

www.ingramcontent.com/pod-product-compliance
Lightning Source LLC
Chambersburg PA
CBHW070623100426
42744CB00006B/593